All's Well That Ends Well

In this beautiful book Peter has married the extraordinary words of Shakespeare to the extraordinary truths of the gospel, so as to touch and bless your life. *Paul Bayes, Bishop of Liverpool*

Peter Graystone's book will bring pleasure and wisdom in equal measure to its readers. He selects from both the familiar and unfamiliar, and provides helpful context and summary, but the heart of this book is the way his commentaries on each piece draw out the relevance and beauty of Shakespeare's poetry for your own spiritual journey. This book is a treasure in itself but will also send you back to the plays with renewed enthusiasm and insight. *Malcolm Guite, poet and singer-songwriter*

In *Desert Island Discs* the two books we're invited to take to our island are the Bible and Shakespeare. Here Peter uses one to help us understand the other. His writing is accessible, informed and thought-provoking, whether you are a wannabe Laurence Olivier or you haven't been near *Hamlet* since school. *Kate Bottley, broadcaster*

Peter loves people, the theatre and Jesus, not necessarily in that order. He has the gift of writing beautifully about them in ways which shed new light for the rest of us. This is a wonderful book. *Stephen Hance, Church of England National Lead for Evangelism and Witness for the Church of England*

All's Well That Ends Well

From Dust to Resurrection –
40 Days with Shakespeare

Peter Graystone

CANTERBURY
PRESS

Norwich

© Peter Graystone 2021

Published in 2021 by Canterbury Press
Editorial office
3rd Floor, Invicta House,
108–114 Golden Lane,
London EC1Y OTG, UK
www.canterburypress.co.uk

Canterbury Press is an imprint of Hymns Ancient & Modern Ltd
(a registered charity)

Hymns Ancient & Modern® is a registered trademark of
Hymns Ancient & Modern Ltd
13A Hellesdon Park Road, Norwich,
Norfolk NR6 5DR, UK

British Library Cataloguing in Publication data
A catalogue record for this book is available
from the British Library

Unless otherwise noted, Scripture quotations are taken from the Geneva
Bible, 1599 Edition, modernised spelling edition. Copyright © Tolle Lege
Press, 2006. Permission sought.

Quotations marked (NIV) are from the Holy Bible, New International
Version Copyright © Hodder and Stoughton, 1973, 1978, 1984, 2011
(inclusive language version, 2001).

Shakespeare quotations are from Open Source Shakespeare, based on
the 1864 Globe edition of the complete works, in the public domain.
(www.opensourceshakespeare.org)

Photographs are by Raewynne Whiteley,
with thanks to the Belvedere Trust.

978-1-78622-354-8

Typeset by Regent Typesetting
Printed and bound by
CPI Group (UK) Ltd

For Laura

It is required you do awake your faith.
The Winter's Tale, Act 5, Scene 3

Contents

Day 1

Golden lads and girls all must, as chimney-sweepers, come to dust

GUIDERIUS AND ARVIRAGUS:
Fear no more the heat o' the sun,
Nor the furious winter's rages;
Thou thy worldly task hast done,
Home art gone, and ta'en thy wages:
Golden lads and girls all must,
As chimney-sweepers, come to dust.

Fear no more the frown o' the great;
Thou art past the tyrant's stroke;
Care no more to clothe and eat;
To thee the reed is as the oak:
The sceptre, learning, physic, must
All follow this, and come to dust.

Fear no more the lightning flash,
Nor the all-dreaded thunder stone;
Fear not slander, censure rash;
Thou hast finished joy and moan:
All lovers young, all lovers must
Consign to thee, and come to dust.

No exorciser harm thee!
Nor no witchcraft charm thee!
Ghost unlaid forbear thee!
Nothing ill come near thee!
Quiet consummation have;
And renowned be thy grave!

Cymbeline, Act 4, Scene 2

We begin with an ending.

These ravishing words are sung at a funeral in William Shakespeare's play *Cymbeline*. Having said that, it turns out not to be a funeral because the young man they are mourning is not dead, but sleeping. And it isn't actually a man, but a woman in disguise. And although they don't realize it, she is their sister. This is, after all, Shakespeare!

Cymbeline is performed less frequently than some of his other works. No one claims that it's a great play, but it has moments of true beauty, such as this. It comes from the end of his career when, after the rage and despair of his tragedies, the tone of Shakespeare's plays turns towards hope. A grace floods in that is recognizably Christian to those who have eyes to see it. This is why he is such fitting company for Lent and over the next 40 days we will journey with him from dust to resurrection.

William Shakespeare lived from 1564 to 1616. It's widely known that he was born on 23 April and died on his birthday. In fact, though, no one knows the date of his birth. What we do know is the date of his baptism. That was on Wednesday 26 April. So it's reasonable to guess that he was born three days earlier. And to think that he might have been born and died on the same day is satisfying in a way that is somehow Shakespearian.

Actually we know relatively little about the life of the man who is routinely described as the greatest writer of all time. The first full biography came nearly three centuries after his birth. A few dozen legal documents about his business have survived – tax returns, property deeds. They tell us where he was living at various times and give a sense of how wealthy he was. There are also references to him in letters by contemporaries which give a clue about how famous he was. But most of his life is an intriguing blank.

We do, however, have a very full record of his work, some of which was published during his lifetime, and then collected into editions shortly after his death. *Cymbeline* was probably performed first in 1610, when theatres reopened after a long period of closure because of the plague. King Cymbeline was a historical figure and ruled south-east England about the time of Jesus. He had good relations with the Roman Empire, but his son did not, which is what caused the emperor Claudius to invade. This battle gives the play its climax, although Shakespeare was no respecter of historical accuracy in this or other plays.

The plot is, frankly, labyrinthine. One of its strands is the story of Imogen, the king's daughter. She marries Posthumus against her parents' will and as a result he is banished. In his adopted home in Rome he speaks devotedly of Imogen's goodness. He is persuaded by his so-called friend Iachimo into a wager over whether it is possible for Imogen to be seduced. Iachimo goes to England and she rebuffs his advances. However, he hides in a trunk in her bedroom and discovers intimate details about her which lead Posthumus to believe that she has slept with him. He is so distraught that he joins the invading Roman army.

Posthumus sends a letter to Imogen asking her to meet him on the Welsh coast where the army's boats will land. This is a ploy since he intends to have her killed. She disguises herself as a boy to make the journey. In Wales she meets Guiderius and Arviragus. Although none of them realize it, they are her brothers who had been kidnapped 20 years before. While they are hunting, she takes what she believes to be medicine but is actually a sleeping potion so effective that when the men return they think she is dead. This is the point at which they sing the funeral song.

Imogen wakes and meets the commander of the invading Roman army. She joins their ranks. The battle goes badly for Cymbeline's troops until Guiderius and Arviragus join the fight and win the day. In defeat, all the men who have wronged Imogen are filled with remorse and repent. Cymbeline summons all the characters for judgement but, one piece at a time, the truth is revealed, disguises are cast aside and joyful reconciliations take place. Instead of executing the Roman leaders, Cymbeline makes peace, declaring, 'Pardon's the word to all.'

One of the reasons the play is interesting is that it repeats ideas that Shakespeare had used in earlier plays, but turns the pain into blessing. A sleeping potion leads to tragedy for the young couple in *Romeo and Juliet* but here, in Shakespeare's final decade, it brings new life. A fractured relationship between a father and his daughter destroys a family in *King Lear*, but here it is healed in time for both to enjoy peace restored. It's as though the ageing playwright cannot bring himself to let hope die.

At the very heart of the play is dust. It's the recurring image in the gorgeous words of the funeral song. There is no hint in these verses of a Christian hope, which is as you would expect of a play set in pagan times. And yet they have a deeply reassuring sense of rest after the tribulation of life.

How has Shakespeare achieved this? The first thing you notice is that it is impossible to read these lines quickly. He has made it so by making use almost entirely of monosyllables – 80 per cent of the words. With the slow pace comes dignity. He has ordered the lines with a simple and regular rhyming scheme. In each of the first three stanzas the first and third lines rhyme, then the second and fourth, and the fifth and sixth. With that orderliness comes the sense that death is not chaotic, but a culmination of life's rhythms.

And in each stanza the lines head towards the same inevitable conclusion – dust. He even incorporates a witticism about sweeping chimneys, which underlines the sadness with a shrug. (Chimney-sweeper was also a regional nickname for a dandelion, which passes from golden to grey before it's blown away.) The final stanza has three pairs of rhymes (or half-rhymes), like an incantation that settles finally into a quiet grave. It's controlled, it's tender and it drives out fear. Beautiful!

Pagan? Yes, of course. But Christians reading this on Ash Wednesday cannot help but associate it with a ritual deeply embedded in their own tradition. On the first day of Lent, Christians gather to have ash imposed on their foreheads in the shape of a cross. Over and again these words are repeated:

'Remember that you are dust and to dust you shall return. Turn away from sin and be faithful to Christ.'

It's an invitation to reflect on our mortality. And in remembering it, to prepare for it through repentance and changed life. Death is going to come to us. That is a reason to live wisely. The golden days of youth and love may distract us, but they cannot change the facts. Neither sceptre (the power of a king) nor learning nor physic (medicine) can altogether prevent it. In the Christian church, the 40 days of Lent start with a death. We begin with an ending.

The Bible story that is frequently told on this day is also about a certain death which is transformed by the intervention of Jesus.[1] A woman is caught committing a sin that she cannot deny. She is dragged into the temple and stands before Jesus, humiliated and terrified. Religious leaders have burst in and found her having sex with a man she isn't married to. They seem gleeful. They know that the punishment laid down in law is that she should be stoned to death. It puts Jesus in a difficult position. The men want to know whose side he is going to take – the Jewish religion, to which Jesus says he is utterly committed, or a vulnerable woman for whom he has great compassion. Whatever he does in this situation, Jesus loses – or so the men think.

Jesus, wonderfully, doesn't do either. Instead he doodles with his finger in the dust of the temple floor. I've known this story for 50 years and I've always wondered what it was he wrote or drew that so dumbfounded the men that they walked away. What was the significance of those words, that picture? This year, reflecting on Shakespeare's poem, something new occurred to me. It wasn't the word he was forming that was significant at all. It was the dust his fingers were in that was the message. That's what he wanted those vindictive men to think about. Life in a handful of dust.

'Remember you are dust and to dust you shall return.' It's so obvious when you've seen it.

---

1 John 8.1–11.

Jesus insists that the men should only throw a stone if they can declare with integrity that they have never sinned. None of them can. Each man walks away. And the woman? 'Turn away from sin and be faithful to Christ.'

This is the journey we will take with William Shakespeare over each of the next 40 days. We'll examine a speech and work out what he wants us to know. We'll find out a little about his life. And we'll trace the path of his ideas into the Bible, which was becoming increasingly accessible in English during his lifetime.

We will keep a good Lent. We will have a Holy Week. And then we will come to Easter with rejoicing, because all's well that ends well. Be ready for some life-enhancing discoveries. 'It is required you do awake your faith.'

Day 2

Love all, trust a few, do wrong to none

THE COUNTESS: Love all, trust a few,
Do wrong to none: be able for thine enemy
Rather in power than use, and keep thy friend
Under thy own life's key: be chequed for silence,
But never taxed for speech. What heaven more will,
That thee may furnish and my prayers pluck down,
Fall on thy head! Farewell, my lord.

All's Well That Ends Well, Act 1, Scene 1

The play that gives this book its title is a problem. From the viewpoint of the twenty-first century, it is an entirely inappropriate name for the play. It ends with all the young characters married, but the chance of lasting happiness coming out of any of those relationships is slim.

Obviously a book about Shakespeare that ends with Easter had to be called *All's Well That Ends Well*. No other title would do! The Christian hope is resurrection. All our endings will be beginnings. As Julian of Norwich wrote two centuries before Shakespeare wrote this play, 'All shall be well, and all shall be well, and all manner of thing shall be well.'[1] But on day two it's fitting to recognize that there are many for whom this Lent is a difficult and perplexing time. It won't end well for everyone. For people in those circumstances, Shakespeare will be a good companion – he has words for them, too.

All's Well That Ends Well begins in France. Helena is given Count Bertram as a husband as a reward for healing the king of an illness. She adores him. He refuses to contemplate the

---

1 Julian of Norwich, *Revelations of Divine Love*, written in 1373.

possibility of a relationship with someone as lowly born as her. So, with a scoundrel as a companion, Bertram goes to Italy and enlists to fight in their wars. He sends a letter saying that he will never acknowledge their marriage unless she is pregnant with his child and has the ring from his finger to prove the baby is his. Bursting with goodness and courage, Helena sets off across Europe to win him back.

She tracks Bertram down to Florence, where he is trying to coax a chaste young woman called Diana into bed. Helena and Diana become friends and Diana shows her the ring that Bertram has given her as part of his seduction. Bingo! Helena disguises herself as Diana and sleeps with Bertram. Kerboom!

Helena fakes her death and the action reverts to France where the court is in mourning for her. Members of the older generation speak words of wisdom and lament. But then everyone arrives from Italy. The truth is revealed. Helena shows that she has fulfilled the conditions Bertram set. He repents and vows to be a worthy husband. Diana is also promised a husband. Even Bertram's good-for-nothing companion is rehabilitated.

'All yet seems well,' the king declares. 'And if it end so meet, the bitter past, more welcome is the sweet.'[2] Personally, I can't see them making it to Mothering Sunday without calamity.

And yet, for all its problems, a fine production of *All's Well That Ends Well* can weave a joyful spell on a stage. It has a fairy-tale quality that begs the audience not to be cynical, but to surrender to the possibility that young people can mature. If a director is able to balance that with emotional depth and show Helena growing from a folklore heroine to a real woman, it can prove to be a colourful, romantic comedy.

The most striking feature of the play is the contrast between the old and the young. There is a group of older people who are carrying the approach of death with resilient insight. The Countess, who makes the speech that begins this chapter, is Bertram's mother and Helena's guardian. Lafew is a member of the French court and is appalled by the reckless behaviour

---

2 Act 5, Scene 3.

of the young people. Diana has a mother, the Widow, who is both kind and sensible.

In contrast, Helena is hopelessly blinded by love. Diana, by enabling that unlikely bedroom deception, confirms the play's low opinion of male sexual behaviour – in the dark all women are alike to men. And Bertram, for all his good looks, is an arrogant cad.

If only Bertram had listened to his mother's advice. Almost nothing that the Countess tells him about love, trust and valuing friendship features in his subsequent behaviour. She tells him to 'be able for thine enemy rather in power than use' (in other words, to win over enemies by good use of power, not by abusing them). And to be 'chequed for silence but never taxed for speech' (meaning to speak neither too little nor too much).

Lists of virtues passed on by parents to children appear quite often in the plays. In the better-known play *Hamlet*, a courtier called Polonius gives similar advice to his son, although he is teased as a windbag for it. It includes spiritual advice that has a biblical ring to it, although it is entirely secular, such as 'Above all, to thine own self be true'.[3]

The reason it sounds biblical is that the New Testament letters also have quick-fire lists of ways to translate Christian faith into everyday behaviour. They are often by Paul, written to churches or individuals for whom he has a role as a guardian. This one has echoes of the Countess' speech:

> Let love be without dissimulation. Abhor that which is evil, and cleave unto that which is good ... Rejoice with them that rejoice, and weep with them that weep. Be like affectioned one towards another: be not high-minded: but make yourselves equal to them of the lower sort: be not wise in yourselves ... If thine enemy hunger, feed him: if he thirst, give him drink: for in so doing thou shalt heap coals of fire on his head. Be not overcome of evil, but overcome evil with goodness.[4]

---

3 *Hamlet*, Act 1, Scene 3.
4 Romans 12.9, 15, 16, 20, 21.

Both Shakespeare and the teaching of the Bible remind us that the qualities we require in order to thrive as Christians, or indeed as humans, are relational. Relationships, whether they are in the community, the workplace or the church, require sincerity, integrity and humility. They break down when we stop talking, but also when we stop listening. They depend on being able to inspire trust and on guarding friendship as attentively as life ('under thy own life's key'). And in both passages the way we treat 'enemies' is crucial to our well-being.

The translation of the Bible quoted here, and all through this book, is the Geneva Bible. Published in 1560, four years before Shakespeare was born, it was the English-language version that he used. So whenever there is a quotation from the Bible during these 40 days, you are reading the same words that Shakespeare read. There was another translation called the Bishop's Bible which was preferred by the government and used in church services. But if there was a Bible in the home, it was more likely to be the Geneva Bible and when Shakespeare alluded to a verse (particularly in later plays like All's Well) he used words that show this was the translation he knew.

It's called the Geneva Bible because that is where Protestant theologians who fled England to escape persecution during the reign of the Catholic Queen Mary took refuge and worked on the translation. It was notable because it was highly readable – it was the first translation to have verse numbers – and almost every paragraph had a comment in a footnote applying the Bible to everyday life. It also had study aids such as maps and tables. Church of England leaders disliked these annotations, leading James I to commission the Authorized Version (or King James Version) to replace it. That was published in 1611 and although it would be pleasing to think that Shakespeare contributed to that translation, he didn't. An edition of the Geneva Bible with modern spelling was made in 2006 and that is the version you are reading in this book.[5]

So we have a play with a title that promises a perfect resolution, but then introduces compromised characters who won't

---

5 Published by Tolle Lege Press, Dallas, TX.

behave as they would in a fairy tale, and delivers a problematic ending. I admit that *All's Well That Ends Well* might not be as good a title as it first appeared for a book like this which is supposed to culminate triumphantly with Easter.

But let's think again about the nature of the resurrection. The Gospel of Mark was the first of the four in the New Testament to be written. Compromised characters and a problematic ending describe that Gospel precisely. This is how it concludes, describing how the women who loved Jesus responded to finding his tomb empty on that Sunday morning: '[They] fled from the sepulchre: for they trembled, and were amazed: neither said they anything to any man: for they were afraid.'[6]

They did not witness the resurrection. They missed it. There were no witnesses to Jesus' resurrection. By the time the women arrived with spices, by the time the stone was rolled away, by the time an angel appeared, it had already happened. Jesus had got on with what only God can do. In the dark of the night, in the silence of the tomb, he had quietly risen from the dead.

Crucifixion is deafening and sickening. Resurrection is the opposite. It happens out of sight and unheralded. When we are suffering and the weight of life seems intolerable, those are the circumstances that most closely resemble the first Easter. Resurrection may already have begun – life returning inside the shroud, inside the tomb.

Trembling, amazed, afraid. Is that really a resurrection experience? It is. We look forward to a time in eternity when the resurrection will be complete. There will be joy and triumph and alleluias. But that is not how the resurrection began. It began with three scared women who didn't know what to say.

Make the most of this unusual journey through Lent and expect surprises. If you arrive at Easter and discover that the burden that life is asking you to carry at present means that you can't share the jubilation that others are experiencing, you are not alone. You are Mary Magdalene, you are Mary the mother of James, you are Salome. 'And all shall be well, and all shall be well, and all manner of thing shall be well.'

6 Mark 16.8.

Day 3

When icicles hang by the wall

HOLOFERNES AND NATHANIEL:
When icicles hang by the wall
And Dick the shepherd blows his nail
And Tom bears logs into the hall
And milk comes frozen home in pail,
When blood is nipp'd and ways be foul,
Then nightly sings the staring owl,
Tu-whit; tu-who. A merry note,
While greasy Joan doth keel the pot.

When all aloud the wind doth blow
And coughing drowns the parson's saw
And birds sit brooding in the snow
And Marian's nose looks red and raw,
When roasted crabs hiss in the bowl,
Then nightly sings the staring owl,
Tu-whit; tu-who. A merry note,
While greasy Joan doth keel the pot.

Love's Labours Lost, Act 5, Scene 2

The earliest surviving reference to any of William Shakespeare's family is a pile of poo. There is a court record dated 1552, 12 years before William was born, of his father John being found guilty of keeping a dung heap in Stratford-upon-Avon, a town in Warwickshire. He was fined one shilling. That's a lot. It was about two days' wages for a glove maker like John Shakespeare. This wasn't just the middle classes being fussy about the state of their neighbours' gardens. The 1550s were the height of the plague years and outbreaks in Stratford were frequent. They were trying to protect themselves.

In a normal year of the sixteenth century, 15 per cent of English children would die in infancy. However, in a plague year it was a third. The years between 1556 and 1559 were terrible in Stratford-upon-Avon. The burial records of Holy Trinity Church list 200 deaths. That was from a total population of only 2,000. Also, the harvest failed in 1556. In many ways it was a dreadful time to be alive. Shakespeare's greatest achievement was not writing *Hamlet*; it was surviving past his first birthday.

Sadness and the presence of death are present in all the plays. That seems perverse to say about the comedies which, in a good production, can make you laugh until you ache. But it is true. *Twelfth Night* ends with joyful reunions and marriages. But the audience's favourite character storms out vowing revenge and the play closes with the jester singing a song as the rain starts to fall. And the sunniest of all the comedies, *Love's Labour's Lost*, ends in the depth of winter with the poem we focus on today.

It's a beautiful evocation of a harsh season. It's so cold that not only the water has frozen, but also the milk. Workers resolutely keep going – no amount of sweat is going to stop Joan stirring her vat of stew. There is so much flu that in church the parson's sermon is drowned out by coughing. Marian has got it so badly that her nose is red with sneezing, hopefully not into the crab apples she's pickling.

And yet there's a surprise. You would expect to hear a mournful bird song to match these bleak conditions. But you don't. Instead you hear the owl singing merrily. And the out-of-place cheerfulness is matched by an unexpected rhyming scheme. Pairs of lines in each stanza rhyme satisfyingly – the first and third, second and fourth, fifth and sixth. Then the closing couplet has a half-rhyme which leaves the poem slightly askew.

Immediately prior to this, there has been a poem about the joy of spring. Flowers are blooming and the young are attracting the attention of the opposite sex. But in that lusty setting, the cuckoo's song is a miserable squawk that sounds just like 'cuckold'. What a let-down!

Love's Labour's Lost is my favourite of Shakespeare's plays. You will read that sentence several times about different plays between now and Easter.

Four young Spanish noblemen declare a solemn oath that for three years they will commit themselves to education and scholarship, renouncing fine food, luxury and (most of all) the distracting allure of women. They manage to keep their vows for about five minutes.

Four young women from the French aristocracy arrive to visit the king. The men are instantly smitten. They each send a letter and gift to one of the women, thinking they are the only ones to break their pledge, but the letters find their way into the wrong hands and conversations are overheard, so they find each other out. In a scene of escalating hilarity, the men disguise themselves as exotic Russians in order to court the princess and her companions. The women are not fooled for a moment, but swop the gifts they have been sent in order to bamboozle the men. All is revealed, the couples pair off and the stage is set for a carefree future of love and contentment.

And then something happens which I won't reveal because if you haven't seen the play it comes as a tremendous shock. It is impeccably dramatized by a playwright who, relatively early in his career, has the confidence to tangle an audience's emotions. That is how the play comes to a close with a song about a blossoming spring, in which the cuckoo screeches a miserable note, and a song about a bitter winter, in which the owl hoots with a defiant hope. Such is life!

'Hope that is deferred is the fainting of the heart, but when the desire cometh it is as a tree of life.'[1] It is reasonable to assume that Shakespeare would have read that proverb from the Old Testament. He knew his Bible! He certainly knew the concept, because so much of the dramatic tension in his plays

---

1 Proverbs 13.12.

comes from watching characters confronting the obstacles to their hopes being fulfilled. 'The miserable have no other medicine, but only hope,' says one of the characters in *Measure for Measure* when he reaches rock bottom.[2]

Hope is one of the great themes of the Bible. In the letters of Paul it distinguishes those who have put their faith in Jesus from those who haven't. Hope can't be measured or held or seen. It can only be sensed deep down with what Paul calls 'the eyes of your heart'. He prays for the Christians of Ephesus, 'that the eyes of your understanding may be lightened, that ye may know what the hope is of [God's] calling, and what the riches of his glorious inheritance is in the saints'.[3]

So what is hope in the Bible and is it any different from the hope which is all that is left at the end of *Love's Labour's Lost*? It's easier to say what hope doesn't mean. It isn't a vague sense of hoping for the best when actually you have no idea what to expect. I hope it's going to be sunny over Easter weekend for the sake of all the couples who are going to get married. But I have no way of knowing whether it will be and there is nothing I can do to influence it. I just have to wait and cross my fingers.

And equally, Christian hope is not a certainty. It deals with things that cannot be proved. I have heard people, even preachers, declare, 'I am certain with no shadow of doubt that there will be a life after death.' But I don't see how it's possible to be certain about things like that. They are a matter of faith, not of proof. If it were possible to be certain then everyone in the world would be believers and, plainly, not everyone is.

I will be straightforward with you. I have come to the conclusion that there is a God, that I will meet him, and that there will be a joyous future beyond my life on earth. All will be well that ends well. But I can't prove it and it would be foolish of me to say that I am certain.

Hope means having a calm and settled state of mind based on the assumption that in everything, from the huge decisions to the smallest, we can rely on God. It is a confidence that we

2 *Measure for Measure*, Act 3, Scene 1.
3 Ephesians 1.18.

can trust him for all the things about which it is impossible to be certain. And that can transform a life. It means that when we have anxieties about what the future holds or doubts about what we believe, they come in the context of a mindset that assumes we have a good God who wants the best for us and is preparing for us an eternity that is consummately rich. 'The riches of his glorious inheritance', as Paul puts it. It can give us courage to endure loss, disappointment and 'the fainting of the heart' with a quiet trust that we are loved by and safe in the hands of God.

We know how *Love's Labour's Lost* ends, but we can only guess what happens next to the characters to whom we have grown very attached. There is a reference in records to a subsequent play called *Love's Labour's Found*, but it did not appear in the collection when Shakespeare's plays were published after his death, so perhaps a sequel is lost. However, the ending we have, in which hope is deferred, is extremely satisfying.

None of us knows how our journey of faith will end either. But we have a Christian hope and that too is extremely satisfying. It got me through last winter. Tu-whit; tu-who.

Day 4

The quality of mercy is not strained

PORTIA: The quality of mercy is not strained,
It droppeth as the gentle rain from heaven
Upon the place beneath: it is twice blest;
It blesseth him that gives and him that takes:
'Tis mightiest in the mightiest: it becomes
The throned monarch better than his crown;
His sceptre shows the force of temporal power,
The attribute to awe and majesty,
Wherein doth sit the dread and fear of kings;
But mercy is above this sceptred sway;
It is enthroned in the hearts of kings,
It is an attribute to God himself;
And earthly power doth then show likest God's
When mercy seasons justice. Therefore, Jew,
Though justice be thy plea, consider this,
That, in the course of justice, none of us
Should see salvation: we do pray for mercy;
And that same prayer doth teach us all to render
The deeds of mercy.

The Merchant of Venice, Act 4, Scene 1

I was at a church service where the prayers began, 'Lord, you have taught us that mercy is twice blessed – it is a blessing both to those who give it and those who receive it.' God has indeed taught us that, although not through the Bible but through Shakespeare's play *The Merchant of Venice*. I suspect the person leading the prayers was muddling the two. This chapter is going to increase the muddle. This is not a delightful play about mercy; it is a disturbing play about money.

In Belmont, Italy, Portia's fabulously wealthy father did his best to warn her about money's corroding influence. Anticipating that gold diggers would woo her for her fortune, he stipulated in his will that her suitors must choose between a gold, a silver and a lead casket. Whoever chooses the right one will marry her, but those who choose the wrong one are destined for lifelong celibacy. As anyone who has ever read a fairy story would anticipate, the one who chooses the lead casket wins the bride because 'all that glitters is not gold'.[1] Sadly, though, Portia's father is dead before the play begins and none of the characters who survive him have a crumb of his wisdom.

In Venice, meanwhile, Bassanio has set his heart on winning her hand and thus her fortune. He pleads with his friend Antonio to lend him enough money to make himself credible to court Portia. Antonio, the merchant of the title, has a crush on him and wants to help, but all his money is tied up in a trade deal and his ships are at sea. He agrees, though, to stand as guarantor for a loan from a moneylender called Shylock. Shylock is Jewish and has no love for Antonio because of anti-Semitic insults he has made. So he makes a deal. He will lend 3,000 ducats without interest, but if the loan goes unpaid, Shylock will be entitled to a pound of Antonio's own flesh.

Three thousand ducats – that's a quarter of a million pounds. Is a human life worth that? The whole premise of the play is that Bassanio needs to borrow money to make himself appear wealthier than he is in order to marry into an even greater fortune. There is precious little love or family warmth. Bassanio marries Portia. But the things that bind people together in relationships in this play are trade deals and debts and inheritances and religions. It's not looking good, is it?

Add in Portia's racism (she dismisses an unsuccessful African suitor by saying that she hopes she doesn't end up having to marry a black man). Plus repeated assertions that to be a Jew automatically implies a lack of any ethical standards. And a

---

1 Act 2, Scene 7.

subplot in which the Christians facilitate Shylock's daughter eloping with one of them and stealing his treasure box. The Christian characters do not come out of this story well.

Dealing with this is a real problem for a director staging the play today. Shakespeare could assume that his audience applauded the worldview of the play, but in the twenty-first century a production that does not recognize and deal with how deeply unpalatable this is will fail. A director cannot make Shylock completely sympathetic either. He has a superb speech which begins by appealing for the humanity of all people to be valued equally: 'I am a Jew. Hath not a Jew eyes? Hath not a Jew hands? ... If you prick us do we not bleed? If you tickle us do we not laugh? If you poison us do we not die?' Its seesawing phrases weigh up the economic value of a life, like goods tipping one way and another on a merchant's scales. But then the true purpose of the speech is revealed. In response to the Christians stealing his riches and his daughter, he will sink to their level of wickedness: 'And if you wrong us shall we not revenge?'[2]

This makes the speech we are looking at today key to the success of a production. A disaster has happened. Antonio's ships have been lost at sea and he cannot repay the debt. Shylock goes to court to demand his death. Portia disguises herself as a lawyer and delivers this bravura appeal for Shylock to show mercy.

This is the point in the play at which ethical values have an opportunity to rise above financial ones. You don't show mercy because you are forced to (it 'is not strained'). You show mercy because you want to bless someone, just like a gentle rain blesses parched earth. And in the endlessly generous economy of God, you end up knowing yourself to be blessed as well. It is the virtue of kings (Shakespeare is alluding to Psalm 72 here. The psalm is a prayer for the king to be just and compassionate towards those who have no one else to help them:

2 Act 3, Scene 1.

19

'He shall come down like the rain upon the mown grass, and as the showers that water the earth. In his days shall the righteous flourish'[3]).

Mercy is at the heart of God's character, pleads Portia, and when humans succeed in holding mercy and justice together, then the power that is being exercised resembles God's own power. If justice were the only quality in God's nature we would all be eternally condemned ('none of us should see salvation'). But we have hope because God is as merciful as he is just and that should be the model for all human action.

This is Portia's attempt to win the moral high ground for the Christians. Shylock does not help himself at this point by cleaning the blade of his knife on the sole of his shoe, like a stereotypical villain. She wins the case. (There is a plot twist which I won't give away.) Shylock is humiliated. The Christians do not show him a scrap of the mercy they entreated from him.

Shakespeare's own audience probably saw this as New Testament salvation conquering Old Testament vengeance. A contemporary audience, however, is more likely to recognize a present-day blight – the system failing to deliver justice to those from a minority and showing the true limits of the regard in which religion is held in a supposedly tolerant society. A production that puts these elements in the spotlight can skewer an audience today as they question their own values – so much so that what could be an extremely unpleasant play is compelling.

The irony is that it is in Shylock's Scriptures, our Old Testament, that the mercy of God is most lavishly described. It is what he most longs that those who turn to him will discover. Mercy pleases God. This is how the prophet Micah expresses it:

'Who is a God like unto thee! ...
He retaineth not his wrath forever, because mercy pleaseth
    him.

---

3 Psalm 72.6.

He will turn again, and have compassion upon us: he will
    subdue our iniquities,
and cast all their sins into the bottom of the sea.'[4]

This is both the Christian hope and the Jewish hope. The Jew-ish woman who was rescued and told to turn away from sin (about whom we read three days ago) found it in Jesus. The Christian making his or her way through Lent will eventually be confronted by the cross on which he died and think again about its cost.

There is nothing easy about mercy. It requires people to dig into their souls and fight their natural desire to get even or restore their wounded pride. When mercy is genuinely offered it cures and helps and heals. However, the relief it brings is almost invariably felt by the one who gives as well as the one who receives. Those who have experienced this (and perhaps only those) know it to be true. 'Blessed are the merciful, for they shall obtain mercy.'[5]

As Jesus said. Or was it Portia?

---

4 Micah 7.18–19.
5 Matthew 5.7.

Day 5

Now is the winter of our discontent made glorious summer

RICHARD: Now is the winter of our discontent
Made glorious summer by this son of York,
And all the clouds that loured upon our house
In the deep bosom of the ocean buried.
Now are our brows bound with victorious wreaths,
Our bruisèd arms hung up for monuments,
Our stern alarums changed to merry meetings,
Our dreadful marches to delightful measures.
Grim-visaged war hath smoothed his wrinkled front;
And now, instead of mounting barbed steeds
To fright the souls of fearful adversaries,
He capers nimbly in a lady's chamber
To the lascivious pleasing of a lute.
But I, that am not shaped for sportive tricks,
Nor made to court an amorous looking glass;
I, that am rudely stamped and want love's majesty
To strut before a wanton ambling nymph;
I, that am curtailed of this fair proportion,
Cheated of feature by dissembling nature,
Deformed, unfinished, sent before my time
Into this breathing world, scarce half made up,
And that so lamely and unfashionable
That dogs bark at me as I halt by them –
Why, I, in this weak piping time of peace,
Have no delight to pass away the time,
Unless to see my shadow in the sun
And descant on mine own deformity.
And therefore, since I cannot prove a lover
To entertain these fair well-spoken days,

I am determined to prove a villain
And hate the idle pleasures of these days.

Richard III, Act 1, Scene 1

Some words written in Shakespeare's own handwriting still exist. To be precise, there are 14. Six of them are signatures. He spells his name in six different ways, none of which is the way we usually spell it today. There is also a handwritten page in the British Library from a play written by several collaborators called *The Book of Sir Thomas More*. Some people think that, late in his career, Shakespeare wrote one of the speeches and that this is his handwriting.

But that's all. It's illustrative of how little we know about Shakespeare the man. It's not the case, either, that the plays lay bare to us a consistent worldview. They are wide open with gaps and into the gaps pour the hopes and fears of each succeeding generation.

For example, productions of *Richard III* always end with the death of the tyrant, but the images that follow it and close the play vary enormously. A production at the end of the Second World War ended with Richard's crown being passed with relief into the safe and peaceful hands of the future Henry VII.[1] A production at the beginning of the twenty-first century ended with soldiers loyal to a platitudinous new king pointing guns at the audience as a military dictatorship took hold.[2] Neither is true to history, but both make sense of the gap that opens up at the end of Shakespeare's play.

The consequence of these gaps is that productions of the plays can be set successfully in the century in which they were written, in modern dress, or in ages past or yet to come. Yet they always seem to be addressing the questions and needs of the present day – never dogmatically; always expansively.

---

1 Laurence Olivier, Old Vic, 1944, subsequently filmed in 1955.
2 Michael Boyd, Royal Shakespeare Company, 2007.

They seem forever topical. Three of the 37 plays actually begin with the word 'Now'.

That includes the one we are looking at today. A horrible man comes on to the stage alone and worms his devious way into our affections. Richard is not yet king at this point. At the end of a ferocious civil war ('the winter of our discontent'), his brother Edward IV is. Edward is the 'son of York', and Shakespeare's original audience would have appreciated a pun, because his symbol was the sun. The sun has come out and driven the clouds away. Peace has taken the place of violence. Dancing has taken the place of marching. Sex has taken the place of combat. Everyone is happy.

No, they aren't. Richard is deeply unhappy. Every word of this speech is spittled with sarcasm. He is playing with the audience. He is seducing us – the first of many people he seduces during this play. He can't dance because he has had a disability since his premature birth ('deformed, unfinished, sent before my time into this breathing world'). He hasn't got the looks to coax a girl into bed ('rudely stamped and want love's majesty'). So he is going to enjoy himself by doing what he knows he is good at – hurting people. 'I am determined to prove a villain,' he sneers. That too has a double meaning – he has made up his mind to be evil, but also it has been determined for him by some sort of supernatural force.

And that's what he does. He kills everyone he has to until he is king. He manipulates a noblewoman called Anne into marrying him. She knows he murdered her first husband, but she lets him persuade her of the political advantages. He piles pressure on the ailing Edward IV by having their brother Clarence executed. When the king dies, Richard becomes Lord Protector until Edward's young sons are old enough to take the throne. He doesn't protect them – he has them imprisoned in the Tower of London and then murdered.

His reign of terror causes the people of England to fear and loathe him. A challenger to his kingship gains momentum from his home in France – the Earl of Richmond. Richard responds by trying to consolidate his power. He has his wife

Anne murdered because marrying the former king's daughter instead would strengthen his claim to the throne. The Earl of Richmond invades. Richard has a dream in which all the people for whose deaths he is responsible curse him. In battle next day, Richard is killed and Richmond is crowned Henry VII.

How much of that is historically accurate? Not much! It is the version of Richard's reign that Shakespeare's patrons, the Tudor monarchs who descended from Henry VII, would have liked to be true. He knew how to please. In actuality, Richard was liked no more or less than other kings. He brought about some good legal reforms. He encouraged foreign trade. It's unlikely that he murdered the princes in the Tower – they may not have been killed at all. He didn't poison Anne – she died of tuberculosis. And although his spine was curved, Shakespeare grossly overplays Richard's disability.

Why was it so important that a villain should be portrayed like that? The only answer is that it responds to something distressing in human nature. It is a feature of fantasy films and literature that has been repeated with depressing regularity. Evil people are ugly or weird (or bald, which is a particular irritation of mine for reasons I won't go into). Voldemort. Darth Vader. Ernst Blofeld. The Joker. The Ugly Sisters. In life too, when a person has been convicted of a grave crime, tabloid newspapers illustrate the story with their most unappealing or distorted photograph. It is as though they are saying to us, 'You should have seen this dreadful thing coming – one look at the face should have warned you there was evil within.'

But evil is not like that. It is often hard to recognize and often hard to resist. Richard III is certainly irresistible. He is charismatic, funny, frank about his vulnerability and lets us into the kinds of secrets that only a best friend knows. When he dies it feels like a tragedy. As well as trashing Richard's historical reputation, Shakespeare elevated him to a heroic level of fascination.

Evil is alluring. But it doesn't look like Shakespeare's Richard III. I categorically reject the image of evil that has horns like a goat and feet like a dragon. The devil does not look like the image you see in medieval wall paintings, tossing people into hell with a pitchfork. We will never see the devil face to face in the way we will see Jesus face to face.

However, there is something about evil that is bigger than the sum of its parts. There is something at large in the world that is working to damage human beings – something more fearful than individual people being villainous. What is it that has conspired throughout human history to make men want to kill each other to gain their land, their wealth, their prestige? What is it about power that means people who have achieved it never want to part with it? What is it about world economics that consistently means that the rich become richer and the poor suffer in consequence? What is it about our nature that means that we seek comfort in our time even when we know that we are creating an environment in which our descendants will struggle to maintain basic human life? This is more than individuals being wicked. There is something spiritual about evil.

First thought: don't speak in a way that's lazy. If you are planning an act of Christian witness in the open air and it rains, that's not because the devil is trying to prevent it happening. That's the British weather. If you are planning to project a film in church and the technology doesn't work, that's not because the devil is attacking. It's because some cable isn't plugged in.

Second thought: don't live in a way that is fearful. Your illness or disability isn't the devil's work. Demons are not going to jump out at you on a dark evening. The devil is not going to work sorcery on your children because they once saw a Harry Potter movie. Be sure of that, because our good and powerful God is the God of the twenty-first century and didn't get helplessly stuck in the Tudor era.

So what should you do instead? Third thought: 'Be strong in the Lord, and in the power of his might,' declared Paul in one of his letters. 'Put on the whole armour of God, that ye may be able to stand against the assaults of the devil.'[3]

3 Ephesians 6.10–11.

Recognize evil for what it is. It is something that is real in our world and leads to tyrants flourishing, half the world dying of trivial diseases for lack of medicines that the other half take for granted, and people being trafficked, enslaved and abused because human wickedness sees them as a means of making money. Be ready to fight it. Paul describes the 'armour' we need in order to confront genuine evil – truth, justice, readiness to seek peace, faith, certainty of our salvation and, above all, the Holy Spirit.

Truth to tell, the ending of *Richard III* is compromised. Richard dies like a tragic anti-hero, desperate to get back into a battle he knows he has lost: 'A horse, a horse, my kingdom for a horse.'[4] But Richmond (the future Henry VII), to whom the crown passes, is an under-developed character. We are not asked to rejoice in his triumph – we enjoyed Richard too much.

Richmond prays about the future: 'God, if thy will be so, / Enrich the time to come with smooth-faced peace, / With smiling plenty and fair prosperous days.'[5] He seems to be praying for the 'glorious summer' which was the state Richard despised in the opening speech. It doesn't bode well for the eradication of evil, does it? When do we need to heed the warning? Now!

---

4 Act 5, Scene 4.
5 Act 5, Scene 5.

Day 6

Romeo, Romeo! Wherefore art thou Romeo?

ROMEO: He jests at scars that never felt a wound.
(Juliet appears in a window above.)
But soft! What light through yonder window breaks?
It is the east, and Juliet is the sun.
Arise, fair sun, and kill the envious moon,
Who is already sick and pale with grief,
That thou, her maid, art far more fair than she.
Be not her maid since she is envious.
Her vestal livery is but sick and green,
And none but fools do wear it. Cast it off!
It is my lady. Oh, it is my love.
Oh, that she knew she were!
She speaks, yet she says nothing. What of that?
Her eye discourses. I will answer it.
I am too bold. 'Tis not to me she speaks.
Two of the fairest stars in all the heaven,
Having some business, do entreat her eyes
To twinkle in their spheres till they return ...
JULIET: Oh Romeo, Romeo! Wherefore art thou Romeo?
Deny thy father and refuse thy name.
Or, if thou wilt not, be but sworn my love,
And I'll no longer be a Capulet.

Romeo and Juliet, Act 2, Scene 2

William was baptized in the Church of the Holy Trinity, Stratford-upon-Avon. The church still stands and the parish register in which it was recorded survives. It's assumed that he was educated at the King's New School, which also stands today.

So he was brought up a Christian. A Protestant Christian. That's significant because the family of his mother, Mary Arden, was Catholic. As if there wasn't sufficient loss of life from disease in that century, successive monarchs added to the death toll for the crime of being from the wrong denomination.

Protestant Elizabeth I had been on the throne for five years when Shakespeare was born. In practice, during her reign it was relatively safe to be Catholic as long as you were openly loyal to her. It was proselytizing for Catholicism that was dangerous. That made writers circumspect and it makes it complicated to find Shakespeare's faith convictions in his writing.

We can, however, find ideologically warring communities in many of the plays. *Romeo and Juliet* sets a love story in the context of two families locked in hatred. It's never clear why the Capulets and the Montagues hate each other, but it's a deeply entrenched feud. Having fallen in love at first sight and unaware that she is being overheard, Juliet Capulet bemoans the fate that will lead to both their deaths: 'Wherefore art thou Romeo?' In other words, why are you Romeo – a Montague – and not from a family of which my parents would approve?

Was telling you that they die a spoiler? No. The play has a prologue and we learn six lines in that the two lovers are going to take their lives. That would not have troubled a sixteenth-century audience. A twenty-first-century audience loves novelty, but theatre-goers in Shakespeare's own time would have rejoiced in the way he reworked stories they already knew.

In the case of *Romeo and Juliet*, some would have been fascinated by the way he used a poem translated from Italian by Arthur Brooke. It was called 'The Tragical History of Romeus and Juliet'. For one small example of the apparently effortless theatrical and poetic skill that Shakespeare brought to adapting his sources, try to imagine Juliet sighing, 'Romeus, Romeus, wherefore art thou Romeus?'

The gorgeous poetry that forms this speech is full of such sighing. It's 'soft' and 'fair' and full of lovelorn exhalations: 'Oh!' It's written in a steady, regular metre like a romantic poem. Each line has ten syllables – five pairs (try saying the first line aloud: 'di dum di dum di dum di dum di dum'). This metre is called an iambic pentameter. Iamb refers to the 'di dum' rhythm and pentameter means that there are five of them. It gives a lofty beauty to the words, like a heartbeat. All the lines are in this metre. Except one. 'Oh, that she knew she were' is shorter. There has to be a tiny pause after it – the heart stops beating. How romantic is that! The disruption of the pattern shows us how important that particular thought is to Romeo.

Did I say this is romantic? I'm going to have to retract that. This is all about sex. It's late at night but it's as if there is no darkness because 'Juliet is the sun.' Two of the brightest stars have had to leave the night sky to go on an errand, so they have asked Juliet's dazzling eyes to 'twinkle in their spheres' until they get back. The reason Romeo wants Juliet to 'kill the envious moon' is that Diana is the Roman goddess of both the moon and virginity. Don't protect your virginity, Juliet, because that will make you 'sick and green'. Romeo is after more than a demure first date. 'Cast it off!' Teenage boys haven't changed much over five centuries.

But the yearning is reciprocated. Later in the play, Juliet is counting the minutes until Romeo arrives: 'Come gentle night, come, loving black-browed night, / Give me my Romeo and when I shall die, / Take him and cut him out in little stars'.[1] To die was Elizabethan slang meaning to have an orgasm. Cutting him into little stars makes sexual ecstasy sound like a little girl doing artwork.

Juliet is 13.

So much happens too early in this play. At the beginning, Juliet's father is arranging her marriage to an unsuitable husband, Paris, and is persuaded to bring the wedding forward from two years hence to the following Thursday. Young men barely out of adolescence die as the feud between the families intensifies. Friar Lawrence, the clergyman who befriends the youngsters, warns them: 'Too swift arrives as tardy as too

---

1 Act 3, Scene 2.

slow'.[2] But then he makes 'short work' of marrying them because he hopes the match will bring about an end to the violence. After the couple sleep together the morning comes far too quickly – they try to persuade themselves that the bird they can hear is the night-time nightingale, but they know it is really the dawn-heralding lark. In order to prevent her from having to marry Paris, Friar Lawrence devises a scheme by which Juliet takes a drug that gives her the appearance of death when she is merely asleep. Romeo finds her and, unable to face life without her, kills himself. But had he delayed minutes, just minutes, he would have seen her wake and the double tragedy could have been prevented.

Too soon, too soon! And Romeo foresaw it: 'I fear too early for my mind misgives, / Some consequence yet hanging in the stars, / Shall bitterly begin'.[3]

To find such sexual passion in the Bible, we need to look at the Song of Songs in the Old Testament. This is how the young woman in that poem is described – does it remind you of anything?: 'Who is this that appears like the dawn, Fair as the moon, bright as the sun, Majestic as the stars in procession?'[4]

Song of Songs is a life-enhancing poem about the goodness of sex as part of God's creation, in which a man and a woman describe each other's beauty as part of their foreplay. At some points in history it has been interpreted as being about the love of God for his people – that is how the Geneva Bible treats it. To be honest, though, that sits awkwardly with the sexy bits. It rejoices in the longing, the loving-tenderness and the intimacy of sex. It suggests some tempting aphrodisiacs. It shows the man and the woman as equals in their desire to give and

---

2 Act 2, Scene 5.

3 Act 1, Scene 4.

4 Song of Songs 6.10. This is how the New International Version renders it. The Hebrew word for 'stars' is ambiguous and could refer to banners. The translators of the Geneva Bible chose the military image 'an army with banners', which suggests that Shakespeare didn't have this verse directly in mind in Romeo's speech.

receive pleasure. It features a wedding celebration and extols the way faithfulness enriches sex.

But most interestingly from the point of view of the play we are thinking about today, it warns against underage sex. Three times there is a plea not to let love be woken up too soon. And to make the point absolutely plain, there is a chorus of friends of the young woman ('the Daughters of Jerusalem') who speak of their determination to protect young girls:

> We have a little sister, and she hath no breasts: what shall
> we do for our sister when she shall be spoken for?
> If she be a wall, we will build upon her a silver palace: and if
> she be a door, we will keep her in with boards of cedar.[5]

Juliet needed the Daughters of Jerusalem. Everyone who watched the play in Shakespeare's day would have known that too. Although a girl in sixteenth-century England could legally be given in marriage aged 12, the average age was 24. For the first audience, the play wasn't a high romance, but a tragedy of youthful impatience.

Lent is a season in which to look at your life as a child of God in all its aspects. Because we are allowing Shakespeare to set the agenda, sex is going to be one of those aspects. This will either be refreshing or alarming if you have only ever connected Lent with forsaking chocolate (of which there is none in Shakespeare). But take the opportunity in God's tender company to consider the place of sex in your past and present life – its presence, its absence; its pleasure, its abuse; the faithful love, the need to protect. All of those are present in *Romeo and Juliet*. And they are all features of sex about which God cares deeply. Rejoice in all that gives light and life. 'Arise, fair sun.' But don't hold back from seeking his loving-kindness if there are scars that haven't fully healed. 'He jests at scars that never felt a wound.'

---

5 Song of Songs 8.8–9.

Day 7

Lord, what fools these mortals be!

PUCK: Captain of our fairy band,
Helena is here at hand;
And the youth, mistook by me,
Pleading for a lover's fee.
Shall we their fond pageant see?
Lord, what fools these mortals be!
OBERON: Stand aside: the noise they make
Will cause Demetrius to awake.
PUCK: Then will two at once woo one;
That must needs be sport alone;
And those things do best please me
That befall preposterously.

A Midsummer Night's Dream, Act 3, Scene 2

Aged 18, William got married to a slightly older woman called Anne Hathaway. She came from a prosperous family who lived in Shottery – walking distance from Stratford-upon-Avon. The Hathaway family home is now a tourist attraction – a beautifully preserved Tudor farmhouse.

They got married in a hurry. We know that because their names appear on a marriage bond. This was not a wedding certificate but a declaration that allowed the couple to skip the reading of the banns and get married straight away. It was expensive. Anne's family must have paid because William's father had gone bankrupt.

Why the rush? Well, they gave birth to a daughter six months later. That may possibly account for it, although being pregnant before you were married wasn't such a big deal in that century. Also, 18 was very young to marry. All the speed has a bit of a shotgun feel to it. There are no clues about the fondness or faithfulness of their marriage. We do know that for most of the 34 years during which they were married, William and Anne lived many miles apart from each other. But for all we know they might have been a doting couple.

A Midsummer Night's Dream has five marriages, or would-be marriages. That's a lot of weddings! Two young girls (Helena and Hermia) end up with two young boys (Lysander and Demetrius). Here's a quiz question for anyone who has seen the play. Can you remember which one marries which? I thought not! We are not really invested in the couples who get married in the same way that we are in other Shakespeare plays. It's the mischief in which they are caught up that captures our imaginations, rather than our fondness for the individuals. The comedy of the mishaps that the four encounter along the way is what makes the play delightful, not the satisfaction of seeing them fall in love. It's not a romantic play; it's a send-up of romantic plays. It's the anti-*Romeo and Juliet*.

And the other marriages? At the beginning of the play, the Duke of Athens is anticipating his wedding to a woman whom he has apparently seized as one of the spoils of a war (extremely unpleasant!). At the end of it, a group of amateur actors make a hilarious muddle of telling the story of two suicidal lovers (highly inappropriate!). In between, a fairy king and queen fight each other because they are both infatuated with an adolescent boy (safeguarding issues!). And the queen has sex with a half-man-half-donkey (you have got to be kidding!).

Most modern productions charge at this imbroglio with pants-down aplomb. It is patently unsuitable for children. Like many others, I first saw it when I was ten. It instantly became my favourite of Shakespeare's plays.

There are three worlds that the characters inhabit and, deep in a wood, they collide. The first world is the Athenian court where a story is established that could, at that stage, lead to either a romantic comedy or a lovers' tragedy. Hermia loves Lysander. Her father wants her to marry Demetrius. Heléna pines for Demetrius, who once loved her. An attempt to elope takes them all into the forest. We are introduced to their world in stately iambic pentameters. 'The course of true love never did run smooth,' says Lysander, in language and metre that could have come from *Romeo and Juliet*.[1]

The second world is that of the amateur dramatics of a group of working-class craftsmen – a weaver, a carpenter and so on. Upon learning that the Duke is getting married and seeking entertainment for his reception, they rehearse a drama. With a mixture of incompetence and big-heartedness, they perform it towards the end of the play. Our favourite among them is Nick Bottom, whose assessment of his own talents hugely, but endearingly, outstrips the reality we observe. The audience can tell immediately how different their lives are from those of the lovers because they speak in prose.

Then there is a different world altogether. The wood is overseen by a frolic of fairies led by King Oberon and Queen Titania. The fairies are capable of both blessing and mischief. Oberon is served by a jester, Puck, whose magic lurches between good intentions, roguery and mistakes. They are introduced with a metre that takes us into an unknown universe, galloping unlike anything we have heard before: 'Over hill, over dale, / Through bush, through brier, / Over park, over pale, / Through flood, through fire, / I do wander everywhere.'[2]

To teach his wife Titania a lesson, Oberon instructs Puck to use a magic flower to make her fall in love with the first thing she sees when she wakes. It is Nick Bottom, whose head Puck has turned into that of an ass. Titania is overcome with lust. She is so enthralled by his 'shape' that we are clearly meant to infer that he is not only eared like an ass, but hung like a donkey. (The expression 'hung like a donkey' comes from the Bible – Ezekiel 23.20. I bet you weren't expecting that to be one of your Lenten discoveries.)

Puck also attempts to sort out the problems of the four young lovers with the magic flower. However, he mistakenly puts it

---

1 Act 1, Scene 1.
2 Act 2, Scene 1.

on the wrong person's eyes, meaning that the men become besotted with the wrong women, the women are incensed and the men get ready for a duel.

In the middle of it all comes the speech we are looking at today. Puck's attitude to the chaos he has caused is glee. He loves it when things 'befall preposterously' and plans to stand back and laugh as havoc ensues. Why would he do this? For the joy of proving what he has observed – that humans are fools.

The irony is that Puck is a fool. He is Oberon's fool. In Shakespeare's plays, a fool is a quick-witted commoner who can puncture pomposity and speak truth to power. Two-thirds of the plays have someone in that role – a jester, a savvy servant or the comic relief in a tragedy. From the very first, audiences loved these characters. The groundlings loved them. They were the workers with cheaper tickets who stood near the stage, and they were able to hear opinions expressed that, if they said them in the wrong company, might get them sacked or worse. But the nobles in the expensive seats loved them too, flattered to hear their lives and morals laughed at.

Puck can make us think about the significance and capriciousness of love, the place of sex in a relationship, whether life is driven by chance or by a supernatural plan, and what we can rely on when darkness threatens to have the upper hand. These are all things that you might hear about in a sermon, but sermons rarely have the same sense of mischief.

A sermon on being a fool would have a lot of scope. The Bible has a great deal to say about foolishness. Repeatedly the Old Testament lambasts people who have become fools – so much so that there are five different Hebrew words that can be translated 'fool'.

It can be used to mean someone who has lost sight of the ways of the Lord, and is therefore gullible and led astray. The introduction to the book of Proverbs explains that it was written: 'To give unto the simple sharpness of wit.'[3]

---

3 Proverbs 1.4.

A different word is used for a fool who responds to instant gratification, no matter how destructive: 'A desire accomplished delighteth the soul: but it is an abomination to fools to depart from evil.'[4] And another for someone whose fine words are not matched by their actions: 'Wise men lay up knowledge: but the mouth of the fool is a present destruction.'[5]

Proverbs derides those who have had an opportunity to come under the influence of godly wisdom, but have scorned it: 'O ye foolish, how long will ye love foolishness? and the scornful take their pleasure in scorning? and the fools hate knowledge?'[6] But the ultimate foolishness is an outright rejection of the Lord: 'The fool hath said in his heart, There is no God.'[7]

This is all a long way from the subversive commentary on society given by Shakespearean fools. And yet there is a foolishness in the New Testament that takes you by surprise and is much more in keeping with Puck's intention to bring blessing through tomfoolery.

Paul, in a letter to the first-century church in Corinth, writes about a spiritual foolishness that defies society's ways. It refuses to participate in things that seem wise to a materialist society. Christians are seen by many to be fools because they don't prioritize wealth and gain, and they don't use force for their personal advantage.

Poor, laughable Christians! Wherever did they get the idea that making themselves weak in this way could gain them anything worthwhile? From Jesus, for whom humiliation and suffering became the way of resurrection and life. 'If any man among you seem to be wise in this world, let him be a fool, that he may be wise. For the wisdom of this world is foolishness with God.'[8]

---

4 Proverbs 13.19.
5 Proverbs 10.14.
6 Proverbs 1.22.
7 Psalm 14.1.
8 1 Corinthians 3.18–19.

One of the ways in which Lent is valuable is that it gives you an opportunity to reflect on how your life appears to others. Are there aspects of the way you live that appear foolish to people because they don't share your faith? Using Puck to shine his mischievous light on your behaviour, ask yourself some questions. Have you done things that prioritize love over financial security? Have you devoted time to things from which you will receive no personal gain, but which benefit vulnerable and dispossessed people?

Have you ever made an ass of yourself because you were driven to it by your Christian convictions? If not, why not?

Day 8

If music be the food of love, play on

ORSINO: If music be the food of love, play on;
Give me excess of it, that, surfeiting,
The appetite may sicken, and so die.
That strain again! it had a dying fall:
O, it came o'er my ear like the sweet sound,
That breathes upon a bank of violets,
Stealing and giving odour! Enough; no more:
'Tis not so sweet now as it was before.
O spirit of love! how quick and fresh art thou,
That, notwithstanding thy capacity
Receiveth as the sea, nought enters there,
Of what validity and pitch soe'er,
But falls into abatement and low price,
Even in a minute: so full of shapes is fancy
That it alone is high fantastical.
CURIO: Will you go hunt, my lord?
ORSINO: What, Curio?
CURIO: The hart.
ORSINO: Why, so I do.

Twelfth Night, Act 1, Scene 1

Music is a way of feeding your longing for the unattainable. It allows you to apprehend what you cannot comprehend.

That's why Christianity, and long before it Judaism, has always been a musical faith. It feeds your longing for love, but it also feeds your longing for exhilaration, consolation, wonder and transcendence. And faith, of course.

All of these are things that are ultimately beyond human capacity. No one has perfect love or perfect wonder, because

39

they fade. No one has perfect faith, because it wavers. But music can take you temporarily to a place where these perfect things seem only just out of reach.

Music makes its first biblical appearance in a genealogy in the opening chapters of Genesis, where the inspiration of musicians is traced back to a man named Jubal (his name means 'ram's horn', which was presumably his instrument of choice).[1] It makes its final appearance towards the end of Revelation where God gives angels harps to sing of his holiness and justice.[2] When the new heaven and new earth are established in all their perfection, music is no longer mentioned, perhaps rendered unnecessary because yearning and longing are over for ever when love, wonder and faith are absolute.

Halfway between the two is a book of 150 psalms whose words are preserved but whose melodies are lost in time. In the psalms, the people of God sing the history of their relationship with the One who is beyond understanding. They feed their identity as God's own with thanksgiving and praise. It must constantly be a brand-new song, because no matter what it accomplishes it will never capture what is inexpressible: 'Sing unto the Lord a new song: for he hath done marvellous things ... Sing praise to the Lord upon the harp, even upon the harp with a singing voice.'[3]

However, alongside those uplifting songs in the book of Psalms are songs of despair and lament. Music does not take away the distress of those who listen or play, but it can ease it. In Psalm 42, the singer likens his search for God to an emaciated deer dragging itself across the desert in a hopeless quest for water. 'As the hart brayeth for the rivers of water, so panted my soul after thee, O God.'[4] (It's the same hart that Orsino is hunting in today's extract, but Shakespeare's pun on heart doesn't work in the original Hebrew of the psalm.) In the middle of the night, the singer remembers old hymns he used

---

1 Genesis 4.21.
2 Revelation 15.1–4.
3 Psalm 98.1, 5.
4 Psalm 42.1.

to sing in the temple and it lifts him: 'In the night shall I sing of him, even a prayer unto the God of my life.'[5] But it can't finally satisfy him and he ends the psalm in as bad a state as he began it: 'Why art thou cast down, my soul? and why art thou disquieted within me?'[6]

People turn to music to feed a desire for love, or for anything that lifts them out of the weight of being human. So the Bible urges us to use music to feed desire. It nourishes a desire for the way of Jesus to saturate the life of a Christian community: 'Let the word of Christ dwell in you plenteously in all wisdom, teaching and admonishing your own selves, in psalms, and hymns, and spiritual songs, singing with a grace in your hearts to the Lord.'[7] It fuels mourning, for example for defeated Israel six centuries before Jesus, which once was a lion but has been enchained and silenced: 'They put him in holds, that his voice should no more be heard upon the mountains of Israel ... This is a lamentation and shall be for a lamentation.'[8] It feeds a yearning for romance in the sexy, passionate Song of Songs: 'The flowers appear in the earth: the time of singing ... is come ... Arise my love, my fair one, and come away.'[9]

It's the romance that Orsino is after in those opening lines of *Twelfth Night*. He is pining for Olivia, but she is so deeply in mourning following her brother's death that she will not even entertain seeing him. He knows that music feeds love, so he wants his musicians to play so much that he overdoses on it ('surfeiting') and ends the ache for ever. There is a beautiful description of how a melody can impact on you – it works the way a breeze takes a scent from a bank of violets and distributes it through the air.

Love is fickle ('quick and fresh'). One moment it is absolutely overwhelming and gives you wonderful emotions that, like the sea, seem boundless in what they can accommodate.

---

5 Psalm 42.8.
6 Psalm 42.11.
7 Colossians 3.16.
8 Ezekiel 19.9, 14.
9 Song of Songs 2.12, 13.

But a minute later it hurts you so badly that everything in life seems worthless ('abatement and low price'). Love ('fancy') can change its shapes so often that you can never be sure whether it is real or 'fantastical'.

Wow! Orsino's got it bad for Olivia. Meanwhile, on the coast of the region of which he is duke, Illyria, there has been one of those theatrical shipwrecks from which people emerge with clothes dry, bones unbroken and relatives missing. Viola has survived but her twin brother Sebastian, who looks uncannily like her, is missing. To survive, she disguises herself as a man, calls herself Cesario, and goes to work for Orsino. She immediately falls in love with him. Orsino sends 'Cesario' to Olivia to tell her he is in love with her. Olivia falls in love with 'him'. Meanwhile, Orsino is unsettled because he is beginning to have amorous feelings for a man, or rather for someone he believes to be a man – Cesario.

So, Olivia desires the unattainable Cesario, Orsino desires both the unattainable Olivia and the unattainable Cesario, Viola desires the unattainable Orsino. Cue music!

Fortunately, in Olivia's house there is a musician to provide it. Feste is the jester and he sings that love is not going to last if you wait (''tis not hereafter') so you should make the most of it while you are young:

> O mistress mine, where are you roaming? ...
> What is love? 'tis not hereafter ...
> Then come kiss me, sweet and twenty
> Youth's a stuff will not endure.[10]

Also in Olivia's household are her servant Maria, her uncle Sir Toby Belch and his friend Sir Andrew Aguecheek (who also has the hots for Olivia). Toby and Andrew live in a state of constant drunken revelry, which incenses the dour and pompous steward Malvolio (and yes, he too is secretly infatuated with Olivia). They, with Maria, set up a plot in which Malvolio

---

10 Act 2, Scene 3.

is tricked into believing that Olivia is in love with him and fantasizes about seeing him grinning incessantly and dressed in yellow stockings with zigzag garters (the scene in which this plays out is one of the most painfully hilarious in all drama).

As if that wasn't enough, Viola's brother Sebastian has survived the shipwreck and is being looked after by Antonio, who is in love with him. As soon as Olivia sees Sebastian, thinking he is the look-alike Cesario, she abandons her mourning and proposes marriage to him.

So then, Malvolio desires the unattainable Olivia, Sir Andrew also desires the unattainable Olivia, Antonio desires the unattainable Sebastian, Olivia desires the unexpectedly attainable Sebastian, but only because she thinks he's someone else. Cue music! Feste sings again.

This confusion is resolved with terrific comic aplomb. Disguises are uncovered and the twins reunited. However, with the exception of Viola, no one really gets what they hoped for at the beginning of the play. Some of them are married, but not to the people they expected; some of them end up alone. Malvolio in particular, who is loved by audiences despite or because of all his failings, realizes how cruelly he has been treated and storms away swearing: 'I'll be revenged on the whole pack of you.'[11] It is typical of Shakespeare's comedies that the ending is not buttoned down with unalloyed happiness. As in life, the joy needs to accommodate awkward elements that don't entirely fit.

The play ends with bittersweet music. Feste sings a final song as the wind picks up and rain starts to fall. He sings about foolishness. When you are young, being reckless seems like a romp. But there comes a point as you grow older when you realize it just means that you're surrounded by drunken tosspots. Is love real or unattainably 'fantastical'? Well, perhaps that's a matter of how you make the best you can of the circumstances you find yourself in, for 'the rain it raineth every day'.[12]

---

11 Act 5, Scene 1.
12 Act 5, Scene 1.

Day 9

I to the world am like a drop of water that in the ocean seeks another drop

MERCHANT: My present business calls me from you now.
ANTIPHOLUS OF SYRACUSE: Farewell till then: I will go
  lose myself
And wander up and down to view the city.
MERCHANT: Sir, I commend you to your own content.
  (Exit.)
ANTIPHOLUS OF SYRACUSE: He that commends me to mine
  own content
Commends me to the thing I cannot get.
I to the world am like a drop of water
That in the ocean seeks another drop,
Who, falling there to find his fellow forth,
Unseen, inquisitive, confounds himself:
So I, to find a mother and a brother,
In quest of them, unhappy, lose myself.

The Comedy of Errors, Act 1, Scene 2

More twins! William's own. His wife Anne was pregnant when they married and Susanna was born in May 1583. The twins Judith and Hamnet were born two years later in February 1585. Susanna grew up to marry a local doctor and the house they lived in, Hall's Croft, still stands in Stratford. Judith grew up without learning to read and made an unhappy marriage to a wine merchant who was cheating on her within a month. Hamnet, sadly, did not grow up at all.

More twins! This time in *The Comedy of Errors*, which was one of the first plays that Shakespeare wrote. Subtle it isn't, but it plays like a dream when a director can mine its great comic potential.

Antipholus of Syracuse takes the audience into his confidence with the rather touching speech we are looking at today. (A speech of that kind is called a soliloquy.) He has come to Ephesus having searched the world over for his long-lost twin and their mother. He has a servant called Dromio. Not only does Antipholus of Syracuse have an identical twin, but so does Dromio and this twin is a servant to (well, what a coincidence!) Antipholus of Ephesus.

Adriana, the wife of the Ephesus Antipholus, takes the Syracuse Antipholus into her home – her mistake and his surprise. But he takes a shine to her sister and starts flirting, which appals both women. Antipholus of Ephesus, locked out of his own home, is arrested for failing to pay for a gold chain which he believes he hasn't received – understandably, because it was delivered to his twin brother instead. The two Dromios try to make the best of the situation as they are sent on errands, shouted at and beaten by the wrong masters.

Adriana comes to the conclusion that her husband's behaviour is so strange that he must be demon-possessed, Ephesus being notorious for its 'dark-working sorcerers' and 'soul-killing witches'.[1] (The original audience, better acquainted with the New Testament than most audiences today, would have recognized this description because Paul finds Ephesus to be a city rampant with sorcery when he visits during a missionary journey.[2]) However, it is the intervention of a Christian holy woman that brings everyone to their senses. The beleaguered pair from Syracuse seek sanctuary in an abbey, where the abbess is a believer in 'wholesome syrups' and 'holy prayers'.[3] Her calm intervention allows all the characters to meet and the truth to be made known. There are further twists to be divulged, but I won't reveal them here for fear that you might possibly begin to question the credibility of the plot!

---

1 Act 1, Scene 2.
2 Acts 19.19.
3 Act 5, Scene 1.

The slapstick hilarity of the action means that there is little room for the inner life of the characters to be explored. That makes today's speech, which comes before the pace grows frenetic, interesting. It's a young man's deliberation about his place in the world. He has a restless soul that cannot find contentment. Who am I? What is my place in the scheme of things? In a world so vast how will I find the person who will love me? The image is rather touching – one drop of water trying to find an identical drop lost in the vastness of an ocean. In failing to find his twin brother he has no identity, merely questions (he is 'unnoticed, inquisitive') and is dissolving into the ocean. All those words beginning with the letter F, 'falling there to find his fellow forth' (it's called alliteration), give a sense of darting around hopelessly in the water.

How does someone find their identity? According to the play, you can find it in a relationship – Adriana later uses the same image of a drop of water inseparable from a sea to describe her marriage. You can find it in what you own – the characters are recognized (or confused) by their gold chains, rings and cash. You can find it in holiness – it takes an abbess to bring the men to the place of integrity they are all seeking, and she promises them 'full satisfaction' when everything has been made plain.[4] But ultimately you find it in recognition – it's the key to being invited in or locked out.

So how does a Christian find the 'full satisfaction' of his or her identity? Through relationship? Partially, because we are created by a God who is three in one, to be people who work towards their completeness in communion with others – in church, in marriage, in society. Through ownership of possessions? Definitely not. Through holiness? Indeed, for we know who we are by discovering the eternal drama in which we are cast and rehearsing our part in it.

Through recognition? Yes, more than any other. The temple of Apollo at Delphi had the words 'Know yourself' inscribed over the entrance, but for Christians the invitation into under-

---

4 Act 5, Scene 1.

standing is: 'Know yourself known by God.' In the New Testament, Paul expresses how our partial self-recognition will ultimately be made complete in the presence of God: 'Now we see through a glass darkly: but then shall we see face to face. Now I know in part: but then shall I know even as I am known.'[5]

More twins! By deception and cunning, Jacob swindles his twin brother Esau out of his rights. It turns a brother into an enemy and Jacob spends his youth on the run. The story is told in Genesis.[6] Jacob seeks refuge with a relative on the far side of a desert. There he prospers, marries and becomes a father. But through all the years he is restless for fulfilment and, after the birth of a son to his first love Rachel, he resolves to seek out his twin and face the consequences of what he has done.

With herds, servants and family, Jacob makes the long journey that will end in a showdown. He sends messengers ahead to ascertain his brother's mood and is alarmed to learn that Esau has gathered an army around him. He dispatches lavish gifts, makes his family as safe as possible, and spends the night alone.

In the dark hours, he confronts a stranger and they fight. The men seem equally matched. The mysterious account encourages us to imagine the stranger wrestling Jacob's head until he has no choice but to look him directly in the face. With that meeting of eyes comes a moment of intense self-understanding. Jacob believes he has encountered the divine. His new insight into the human condition is so significant that he calls the place the Face of God (in Hebrew, '*Peniel*'). In acknowledgement of the insight into his identity he receives a new name. He is no longer Jacob, which means 'taking someone else's place', but Israel, which means 'striving with God'. But the event scars him and he never walks with ease again.

The following day, Jacob can delay the meeting with Esau no longer. The storyteller ratchets up tension, preparing the

5 1 Corinthians 13.12.
6 Genesis 25.19—33.11.

reader to expect carnage. Jacob limps towards his brother, bowing lower with each step. He feels the terror of Esau charging towards him and his hairy arms crashing down on him with their sickeningly familiar smell. But then he realizes that the hands are not strangling him, but embracing him.

Esau raises Jacob to his feet and they weep together for the wasted years. As they look at each other, Esau says something intensely significant for all who want to understand their place in the world – that we will recognize the face of God when we look at the face of another human being and know ourselves to be at peace with them: 'I have seen thy face, as though I had seen the face of God, because thou hast accepted me.'[7]

The weight of significance of this quest for human identity is too heavy for the froth of *The Comedy of Errors* to bear. It's a romp, not a thesis. But after two hours of joyful confusion are resolved, we are left with a young writer's sense of optimism that the world is in the hands of an orderly God. All the characters head into the church and the final words are: 'We came into the world like brother and brother / And now let's go hand in hand, not one before another.'[8] They are spoken by Dromio of Ephesus. Or is it Dromio of Syracuse? It's one of the two.

---

7 Genesis 33.10.
8 Act 5, Scene 1.

Day 10

What need we have any friends if we should ne'er have need of 'em?

TIMON: The gods themselves have provided that I shall have much help from you: how had you been my friends else? Why have you that charitable title from thousands, did not you chiefly belong to my heart? I have told more of you to myself than you can with modesty speak in your own behalf; and thus far I confirm you. O you gods, think I, what need we have any friends, if we should ne'er have need of 'em? They were the most needless creatures living, should we ne'er have use for 'em, and would most resemble sweet instruments hung up in cases that keep their sounds to themselves. Why, I have often wished myself poorer, that I might come nearer to you. We are born to do benefits: and what better or properer can we call our own than the riches of our friends? O, what a precious comfort 'tis, to have so many, like brothers, commanding one another's fortunes! O joy, e'en made away ere 't can be born! Mine eyes cannot hold out water, methinks: to forget their faults, I drink to you.

Timon of Athens, Act 1, Scene 2

Timon of Athens is not performed as frequently as Shakespeare's other tragedies and, to be honest, it isn't as good. It's a play about a man who tries to buy friendship and, when that fails, turns on the world in rancour.

Some people think the play that we have isn't finished. That might account for the fact that several scenes leap from poetry to prose (like today's speech) and back again. The ending fizzles out, which gives the impression that Shakespeare planned to

49

do more work on it. Some people think it was a collaboration between Shakespeare and another playwright – a very successful writer called Thomas Middleton. Some scenes are more reminiscent of his style and vocabulary, including the one from which this speech about friendship is taken. Either way, it doesn't seem to have been performed during Shakespeare's lifetime. An adaptation was staged about 70 years after it was written, but it was over 150 years before there was a performance of the complete text.

Timon is a wealthy and generous businessman. He believes friendship means giving lavishly to people without expecting anything in return. He is a patron of the arts, he pays for people to be released from the debtor's prison and he throws a sumptuous banquet so that he can enjoy people's flattery. He has even borrowed money to fund his munificence. (In this he is like King James I and Shakespeare may have been commenting satirically on his own age.)

Timon has a loyal servant, Flavius, who realizes that he is heading for a financial calamity but isn't listened to when he tries to restrain his master. He breaks the news to Timon that his entire fortune has gone. There are creditors at the door demanding to be paid. Timon is sure that those to whom he has been generous will reciprocate in his hour of need, so he sends servants to ask his banquet guests to help. One after another they turn him down. They were not so much friends as parasites. Furious at this betrayal, Timon throws another banquet, to which they all come. But when the food is uncovered, it is just steam and stones which Timon flings at them before he abandons Athens, cursing humanity.

Meanwhile, someone else also has reason to detest Athens. The soldier Alcibiades confronts the Senate in an attempt to overturn a draconian death penalty that has been imposed on one of his junior officers. When he refuses to quit, he is banished. He leaves Athens enraged and vowing revenge.

Timon, now a vagrant, takes shelter in the woods. He refocuses his energy from generosity to bitterness and prays to the Greek gods: 'Grant, as Timon grows, his hate may grow / To the whole race of mankind, high and low! Amen.'[1] But while out searching for food, he uncovers a hidden trove of gold. Suddenly, he is a very rich man again. This time, though, he plans to use the money to spread misery. When word of his discovery gets around, he is revisited by his false friends, but their hopes of reward are dismissed in a misanthropic salvo.

There are two exceptions. He cynically gives Alcibiades sufficient money to raise an army which will destroy Athens. And when his faithful servant arrives, Timon recognizes that he is the only person who was a true friend to him. Flavius leaves with money, but cannot persuade his master to return with him. The play ends abruptly with Alcibiades ready to attack the city and he announces the news of Timon's death in the forest.

Today's speech, about what friends are for, is full of irony because Timon puts such confidence in the very things that will let him down. It comes at the beginning of the play when his generosity is in full flow. He has just given someone enough money for him to be able to get married. His analysis of friendship is that it is at its most precious when friends help one another: 'What need we have any friends, if we should ne'er have need of 'em?' A friend who doesn't offer help is like a musical instrument that is only looked at, never played. However, Timon hasn't noticed that all the friendship in his circle is one-sided. When he finds tears in his eyes because of his happiness ('mine eyes cannot hold out water, methinks'), the audience has a hunch that more tears will be shed later – for a different reason, methinks!

Both Timon and Alcibiades were historical characters from about 400 years before Jesus who had stories a little like those that Shakespeare told. But tales of fair-weather friends are as old as storytelling itself. Although the Old Testament has stories of people who were let down by friends (Job, for instance), the Bible is extremely positive about friendship.

---

1 Act 4, Scene 1.

Timon would have recognized many of the statements in the book of Proverbs, but sometimes it is not clear what their intention is. For instance: 'A man's gift enlargeth him, and leadeth him before great men.'[2] All Timon's hangers-on found that to be true, but is it a good or bad thing? They would only know if they also read the nearby condemnation of bribery: 'A wicked man taketh a gift out of the bosom to wrest the ways of judgment.'[3]

So what makes a true friend? This is something that we need to dwell on in a generation that allows you to declare someone to be a friend with one click of a Facebook button. For a start, friendship of real value involves a willingness to share honest truth at a deep level. More from Proverbs: 'As ointment and perfume rejoice the heart, so doth the sweetness of a man's friend by hearty counsel.'[4] That was Flavius' approach. He knew that you don't buy wisdom with money, but with loyalty that doesn't waver when circumstances are difficult. 'A friend loveth at all times; and a brother is born for adversity.'[5]

True friends find ways to be open with each other without damaging the relationship, even when they need to be critical. Indeed, constant flattery is not a sign of friendship at all: 'Open rebuke is better than secret love. The wounds of a lover are faithful.'[6] That kind of honesty, even though it stings initially, makes you a better person: 'Iron sharpeneth iron, so doth man sharpen the face of his friend.'[7]

The advice about friendship in Proverbs seems to anticipate our own generation, in which siblings and children may live a great distance away: 'A man that hath friends, ought to show himself friendly: for a friend is nearer than a brother ... Thine own friend and thy father's friend forsake thou not ... for

---

2 Proverbs 18.16.
3 Proverbs 17.23.
4 Proverbs 27.9.
5 Proverbs 17.17.
6 Proverbs 27.5, 6.
7 Proverbs 27.17.

better is a neighbour that is near, than a brother far off.'[8] We need to take friendship seriously because the day will come when we need urgent help and a friend who can be physically present is a godsend in a way that an image of a relative on Zoom can never be.

Perhaps Timon's most basic problem, though, was that a friend who is trying too hard to be upbeat and gregarious can be a pain in the neck, especially when you're trying to get some sleep: 'He that praiseth his friend with a loud voice, rising early in the morning, it shall be counted to him as a curse.'[9]

Somewhere in today's so-so play, or today's great book of the Bible, are ideas that are helpful as we consider our own friendships. Or maybe they are to be found in the way the ideas of the two bounce off each other. That would be most pleasing of all.

---

8 Proverbs 18.24, 27.10.
9 Proverbs 27.14.

Day 11

I'll be thy beadsman, Valentine

VALENTINE: Cease to persuade, my loving Proteus:
Home-keeping youth have ever homely wits.
Were't not affection chains thy tender days
To the sweet glances of thy honoured love,
I rather would entreat thy company
To see the wonders of the world abroad,
Than, living dully sluggardized at home,
Wear out thy youth with shapeless idleness.
But since thou lovest, love still and thrive therein,
Even as I would when I to love begin.
PROTEUS: Wilt thou be gone? Sweet Valentine, adieu!
Think on thy Proteus, when thou haply seest
Some rare note-worthy object in thy travel:
Wish me partaker in thy happiness
When thou dost meet good hap; and in thy danger,
If ever danger do environ thee,
Commend thy grievance to my holy prayers,
For I will be thy beadsman, Valentine.

Two Gentlemen of Verona, Act 1, Scene 1

Piecing together the story of William Shakespeare's life is like playing 'What's the time, Mr Wolf?' We turn and get a frozen view of where he is at a particular moment – his baptism, his wedding, the birth of his children. How he got from one point to another is a mystery. And the biggest mystery is the seven years that follow 1585.

In that year we know he is 21, poor, and newly the father of twins in Stratford-upon-Avon. After that, there are no sight-ings of him until 1592, when he is in London. That's two days' journey by horse, or four on foot. He is wildly successful and he is an actor. What on earth happened to make a country lad leave his family and pursue a career on the stage for which nothing in his young life had prepared him?

There are plenty of guesses about the lost years. Did he travel in Italy, giving him information about the cities that would feature in his plays? Did he go to sea? Was he secretly a Catholic and accompanied priests to the safer north of England? None of these account for an unexpected love of the stage.

Living so far from London, where did he first see a play performed and sense the thrill of being an actor? Theatres in the capital were closed often during those years because of the plague and companies took their shows on tour, so it is possible that a company visited Stratford-upon-Avon. It's known that in 1587 the Queen's Men were in Thame, 60 miles from Stratford. We don't know anything about their performance, but we do know that one of the actors killed another one in a brawl. Might they have been short of an actor by the time their tour was seen by a stage-struck young man in Stratford? It's all speculation.

The reason we know he was in London in 1592, and considered a fine actor, is that he received one of the worst reviews in history from a jealous rival called Robert Greene: 'There is an upstart crow, beautified with our feathers that, with his tiger's heart wrapped in a player's hide, supposes he is as well able to bombast out a blank verse as the best of you. He, being an absolute Johnny-Do-It-All, is in his own conceit the only Shake-scene in the country.'[1]

That is some harrumph! Greene was on his death-bed when he wrote it so he must have needed to get it out of his system. There was evidently a fuss because his publisher wrote an apology to William three months later.

And what of the family back in Stratford-upon-Avon? We know William sent money back home and bought property

---

1 *Upstart Crow* became the title of a BBC television sitcom about Shakespeare's family, in which Robert Greene is a character.

there when he became wealthy, but we can only guess whether he visited or had any part in his children's upbringing. It's possible that Anne had never seen one of his plays when he retired to Stratford in 1611. They did, however, stay married for 34 years, which is a long time for them both to reflect on love, friendship and loyalty. ⁄

Those are the themes of *Two Gentlemen of Verona*, which must have been written soon after Shakespeare arrived in London. Today's extract is the very beginning of the play. Valentine is setting off for a gap year because he wants to see 'the wonders of the world abroad'. His best friend Proteus wants him to stay in Verona, where Proteus is in thrall to 'the sweet glances of thy honoured love', who is a girl called Julia. But Valentine can't stand the thought of wasting away his youth 'dully sluggardized at home'. Rather sweetly, Proteus hopes that whenever Valentine sees something 'note-worthy' on his travels, he will think how much his friend would like to be discovering it alongside him. He promises to pray faithfully for him whenever he uses the beads of a rosary: 'I will be thy beadsman, Valentine.'

Lovely! Hmm! Proteus turns out to be an absolute scumbag.

The play is about the value of friendship and how it compares with the love of a man and a woman. Friendship, particularly between two men, was regarded very highly in Elizabethan times. Literature of Shakespeare's time celebrated love between men as pure because it was not complicated by sexual attraction. It was, after all, a devoted choice. In contrast, a relationship between a man and a woman might have nothing to do with choice or feelings, especially in a wealthy family. It would be more to do with marriage prospects, which had implications for economic security, procreation and family bonds.

Valentine sets off for Milan, where he falls in love with Silvia. This is much against the wishes of Silvia's father, the Duke, who locks her in a tower. Proteus stays in Verona, courting Julia, but his plans change when his father insists that he too must go to Milan. The lovelorn Julia disguises herself

as a boy to follow him. But when she gets to Milan, she discovers that Proteus has forgotten her and is also besotted with Silvia. Determined to win him back, she enters his service as a page-boy. Proteus betrays his friend Valentine by telling the Duke that he is plotting to elope with Silvia and Valentine is banished.

Valentine makes his way to one of those Shakespearian forests where the normal rules don't apply and there is an opportunity for hearts and minds to change. There he meets a group of outlaws, who have similarly been banished, and becomes their leader. Silvia escapes the tower and goes after Valentine. She is captured, but Proteus finds her and rescues her from danger. However, she then finds herself in an even worse position because he declares his love for her and, when she rebuffs him, threatens to rape her.

The way this is resolved is controversial. There are heroic interventions, revelations, declarations of repentance, and at one point Valentine affirms his loyalty to Proteus so vigorously that he appears willing to walk away from his marriage to Silvia rather than lose their friendship. The women are treated terribly but don't seem perturbed that the two gentlemen of Verona do not behave like gentlemen.

Directors have a challenge to make the ending seem satisfactory to a twenty-first-century audience. But they are aided by a series of comical minor characters, the servants of the noble friends and lovers, who describe their romantic entanglements in a much more earthy and authentic way. One of them, Proteus' servant Lance, has a dog called Crab who steals every scene in which he appears. Of all the relationships in the play, the one between Lance and his dog seems the most steadfast. He loves Crab so much that he takes a beating instead of the mutt when it's discovered that someone has weed on the Duke's floor.

The changed expectations since Shakespeare's day of what marriage involves make it hard to appreciate the way the relationships are resolved. The displays of loyal affection that spring to mind are not between married couples. (That is true

of the Bible as well as Shakespeare.) The joys of marriage are usually financial stability, security, sex, children or social standing. The joy of tender devotion is found elsewhere.

It's found in the Old Testament between the future King David and Jonathan, the son of his enemy: 'The soul of Jonathan was knit with the soul of David, and Jonathan loved him as his own soul.'[2] Sometimes readers of the Bible today confuse this with homosexual desire, but that mistake would not have been made by an audience who had watched Valentine and Proteus tolerate each other's faults and value their friendship above anything else.

It is found in a very moving way between Ruth and her mother-in-law Naomi, a century before David. Naomi and her family leave Bethlehem in a time of famine and become refugees in Moab. Her sons marry, but all the men in the family die. Naomi sets her heart on returning to her homeland and expects to leave her daughter-in-law Ruth behind in the security of Moab. But Ruth's affection for Naomi is so intense that she decides to leave everything she knows and throw in her lot with her.

They arrive in Bethlehem destitute – a widow and a foreigner. Naomi's husband Elimelech had rights on some land, but she will be forced to forgo it unless she can find a male relative of his who will assert her claim. Such a man does exist – a farmer called Boaz. It is harvest time and Ruth goes to his fields to gather whatever is left over from the reaping. Boaz notices her and protects her from the workmen, who might consider her fair game.

When Naomi finds out that Boaz has spoken kindly to Ruth, she whispers some secrets about how a woman can find her way into a man's heart and that night sends her to where Boaz is sleeping. When Ruth returns to Naomi the next morning with a shawl full of barley, a gift from Boaz, she knows that his intention is marriage. Boaz purchases the land from Naomi and he and Ruth are married.

---

2 1 Samuel 18.1.

Like *Two Gentlemen of Verona*, it is not an easy story to appreciate because the romance is not connected with the marriage, which is a matter of land and the birth of an heir. Instead the romance is in the kindness of a powerful man and in the loyalty of Ruth to Naomi: 'Thy daughter-in-law which loveth thee, hath borne unto him, and she is better to thee than seven sons.'[3]

If we are going to be challenged about our own kindness and loyalty from either the play or the Old Testament, we need to relocate those values to our very different circumstances. There might be questions to ask about our family relationships, our marriages, our friendships. We might need to ask ourselves whether the importance we have conferred on one has obscured the value of another. In Proteus' case, his sex drive makes him lose all sense of proportion about his other relationships. 'In love, who respects friend?' he scoffs. Silvia cuts him down: 'All men but Proteus.'[4]

But it might not be sex that diminishes the significance of relationships that should be important to us. It could be that a busy life makes it hard to find space in which to communicate with a distant parent. It could be that a demanding family squeezes out a needy friend. It could be that a busy job creates a blindfold that hides an underappreciated spouse. Or maybe it's simpler than that – someone whose company was once life-enhancing has drifted away for lack of effort.

Let the gorgeous words of Ruth to Naomi speak into whatever relationship needs your attention today: 'Whither thou goest, I will go: and where thou dwellest, I will dwell: thy people shall be my people, and thy God my God.'[5]

---

3 Ruth 4.15.
4 Act 5, Scene 4.
5 Ruth 1.16.

Day 12

*O God! methinks it were a happy life to be
no better than a homely swain*

HENRY VI: O God! Methinks it were a happy life,
To be no better than a homely swain;
To sit upon a hill, as I do now,
To carve out dials quaintly, point by point,
Thereby to see the minutes how they run,
How many make the hour full complete;
How many hours bring about the day;
How many days will finish up the year;
How many years a mortal man may live.
When this is known, then to divide the times:
So many hours must I tend my flock;
So many hours must I take my rest;
So many hours must I contemplate;
So many hours must I sport myself;
So many days my ewes have been with young;
So many weeks ere the poor fools will ean:
So many years ere I shall shear the fleece:
So minutes, hours, days, months, and years,
Pass'd over to the end they were created,
Would bring white hairs unto a quiet grave.
Ah, what a life were this! How sweet! How lovely!

Henry VI Part 3, Act 2, Scene 5

'Study to be quiet, and to meddle with your own business, and
to work with your own hands, as we commanded you. That ye
may behave yourselves honestly towards them that are with-
out, and that nothing be lacking unto you.'[1]

1 1 Thessalonians 4.11, 12.

Make it your ambition to live a quiet and simple life was Paul's advice in a letter to a church he had visited in Thessalonica a year or two earlier. It's an ironic entreaty, given that during the visit he had been the cause of a riot. Perhaps it revealed to Paul a longing within himself.

A life of useful activity and only modest achievements is a good life. The things that are important are the respect that people who don't share your Christian faith have for you ('them that are without') and not being in thrall to negative influences ('nothing be lacking'). It's a rejoinder to people who think that a successful Christian is one who has had promotions, influence and acquisitions.

Today's speech is by a king who, burdened by the huge responsibility of having led his nation into war, longs for the quiet and simple life that was never destined to be his.

Henry VI is a trilogy of plays written by Shakespeare shortly after he arrived in London. He seems to have had a period of feverish activity in 1591 and 1592, both as an actor and a writer. *Henry VI Part 1* is assumed to be the play referred to by a theatrical impresario called Philip Henshawe, who kept a diary which is now a valuable source of information about what the experience of going to the theatre was like. He built the Rose Theatre and records the triumph of a play called 'Harey VI'. It took 3 pounds 16 shillings and 8 pence during its first season. That's about £700 today, suggesting large audiences. General admission to stand near the stage cost one penny, dropped into a box (which is how we get the term 'box office'). An extra penny bought you a seat and a cushion. Most new plays were performed three times in quick succession and then rested for several months. However, William's play was performed 13 times in the spring of 1592.

Henry VI had become King of England as a baby about 170 years before the play was performed. As a monarch he was either humble and saintly or weak and ineffectual, depending on your point of view. *Part 1* of *Henry VI* deals with the political machinations that led up to the Wars of the Roses, a series of civil wars for control of the English throne. Noblemen gather in the Temple Garden outside parliament and quarrel over a small point of law. The House of Lancaster (the ruling family – Henry's father was the heroic Henry V) pluck red roses from a bush to symbolize their opinion. The House of York (the family from whom future kings such as Richard III would come) pluck white roses. One of the lords predicts that this trivial argument will one day escalate and cause thousands of deaths.

As the political system is torn apart by petty jealousies, a series of military blunders means that the territories in France that were gained by Henry V are lost by his son. Joan of Arc is a fiery presence in the play, rallying the French. It's a very unsympathetic portrayal, though, showing her as heretical, devious and demonic. The play ends with a brittle peace between England and France and the marriage of Henry to Margaret, the daughter of a French earl.

Henry VI Part 2 shows how armed conflict becomes inevitable because Henry is not strong enough to address the disunity of the country. Nobles are set against nobles. The honourable Gloucester, who had been protector of the country when Henry was an infant, is murdered. Henry's wife Margaret has an affair with Suffolk and they plot to take control.

Then the nobles are set against the commoners, who considered Gloucester to be their champion. They look to a new leader, Jack Cade – a working-class rebel. He inspires an uprising with a particular vendetta against people who can read and write, before coming to a bloody end. The nobles completely fail to understand the commoners. When Suffolk, in disguise on a boat, is captured by sailors, he announces who he is and insists with irritation that nobody so lowborn can possibly kill him. They do, of course. The play ends with Henry on the run and civil war inevitable.

Part 3 deals with the horrors of that conflict. The Duke of York has a claim to the throne and Henry lamely agrees that he will make him heir if he will allow him to continue his reign until he dies. But York is being urged to seize the crown by force. Margaret too has troops loyal to her and fights York so that her son will succeed to the throne. She stabs him to death, but York's sons take up the fight in which they will eventually triumph.

Alongside all this comes the rise of Richard, who is a fierce supporter of the House of York and will become the future Richard III. He is physically disabled and convinced that he will therefore not succeed with women or in the politics of the court. The only way he can see to make a success of his life is to seize the throne, despite the fact that it will require the death of many with a stronger claim. It is Richard who finally kills Henry in the Tower of London.

Shakespeare, still developing his craft as a playwright, already knows how to dramatize scenes in such a way as to give a succession of brutal historical events an emotional grip. For instance, at the height of battle, Henry watches a soldier drag a corpse to a place where he can strip the armour and loot the pockets. As he takes off the helmet he realizes that the man he has killed is his father. Weeping, the soldier wonders how he can possibly tell his mother what has happened. This is the event that brings home to Henry the real cost of his inability to address the strife between his nobles.

No wonder he reflects that he would rather be a simple rural worker ('homely swain'). In his monologue he imagines himself sitting on a hill whittling wood to make a sundial. With it, he would watch minutes become hours and days become years. In this carefree life, his only worry would be to divide time up appropriately between the welfare of his animals, sleep, prayer and fun. In the repetition and constant pace of the lines we can hear the seconds tick genially by ('how many hours ... so many hours' – the technical name for this repetition is anaphora). Living in such simplicity he could expect to grow old ('white hairs') and experience a non-violent death ('quiet grave').

This vision of working life is, of course, absurdly over-romanticized in Henry's imagination. It doesn't take into account hunger, coping with ill-health without medical attention or the trauma of powerlessness. Those issues did not go away over the next four centuries. But the illusion that there is a better life that could have been ours if only the dice had fallen differently is persistent in human nature.

In the Bible, the book of Ecclesiastes comments on it. Henry would have agreed with this analysis, that life is so hard that there is no point in attempting anything more grandiose than to enjoy your food and your work:

> What hath man of all his travail and grief of his heart, wherein he hath travailed under the sun? For all his days are sorrows, and his travail grief: his heart also taketh not rest in the night: which also is vanity. There is no profit to man, but that he eat and drink, and delight his soul with the profit of his labour.[2]

There are words of Jesus, too, which chime with Henry imagining himself counting out working days one by one. He commended a life in which worry about the future is committed into God's hands: 'Care not then for the morrow, for the morrow shall care for itself: the day hath enough with his own grief.'[3]

It is possible to cultivate the quiet ambitions that Paul commended to that church in Thessalonica. Practise being content with a simple approach to life. Practise lying in bed at the end of the day reflecting on any good things that have happened and register that they are part of the world that God has spread before us. Practise looking at your meal before you eat it, with all its smells and tastes and colours, and thank God that he conceived such a sensual world for us. Practise focusing on what you enjoy about people, thanking God that friendship and pleasure are possible in his good world.

There is an irony in Henry's story. He does get the chance to see out his days unburdened with the role of king. But he forgoes it. He is in prison and is liberated by nobles loyal to him. When he is offered the crown once more, he takes it. However, what he actually wants is the trappings of being king

---

2 Ecclesiastes 2.22–24.
3 Matthew 6.34.

without the responsibility. He announces that he will live out of the public eye with a king's privileges and comfort, while his rescuers will become Lord Protectors of England. It's a disastrous decision that will be the death of him.

Simplicity and responsibility are both gifts of God. To take the opportunities offered by the circumstances in which we find ourselves and live them 'to the end they were created' is a godly and worthy invitation. 'Ah, what a life were this! How sweet! How lovely!'

Day 13

Let me not to the marriage of true minds admit impediments

Let me not to the marriage of true minds
Admit impediments. Love is not love
Which alters when it alteration finds,
Or bends with the remover to remove:
O no! it is an ever-fixed mark
That looks on tempests and is never shaken;
It is the star to every wandering bark,
Whose worth's unknown, although his height be taken.
Love's not Time's fool, though rosy lips and cheeks
Within his bending sickle's compass come:
Love alters not with his brief hours and weeks,
But bears it out even to the edge of doom.
   If this be error and upon me proved,
   I never writ, nor no man ever loved.

Sonnet 116

Plague closed the theatres again in 1593. Shakespeare once more drops out of sight. Some people suggest he might have travelled in Europe. We do know for sure, though, that he was writing poetry. In April of that year he published 'Venus and Adonis', a long narrative poem. It was very popular in its time. It's about Venus, the goddess of love, setting her heart on Adonis, who is only interested in hunting.

However, the poems that have captivated Shakespeare's readers ever since are his sonnets, of which this is one. A sonnet always has 14 lines. Shakespeare's usually fall into sections – the first four lines (a quatrain), then a further group of four lines, then another, and lastly two lines that rhyme (a couplet). They typically have ten syllables in each line – five iambic pentameters.

He is too good a writer to be trapped by his own rules, though, so there are exceptions. You can see that here. The first line doesn't have the expected di-dum, di-dum, di-dum, di-dum, di-dum rhythm. The very first word has the emphasis instead of the second word. That was deliberate. He could easily have chosen to write with the expected rhythm: 'I will not to the marriage of true minds.' Instead he begins with a stressed word: 'Let me not to the marriage of true minds.' The result is that we sit up and take notice. He is being insistent. That's clever writing.

So what does Sonnet 116 mean? This is a poem about married love. We know that because he makes reference to the banns of marriage that precede a wedding, in which a congregation is asked: 'If any of you know cause or just impediment why these two persons should not be joined together in holy matrimony, ye are to declare it.'[1]

It's a joyous affirmation of the value of staying constant in a relationship through thick and thin. You know you have found true love if it doesn't change when circumstances change ('alters when it alteration finds'), and doesn't waver when the person you love has gone ('the remover'). 'Love' and 'remove' are half-rhymes. There are several in the sonnet and their slight awkwardness is very appropriate for a poem about the way that love endures even though not everything is going to be perfect.

Enough negatives! The second quatrain changes to positives. Love is a rock-solid lighthouse around which waves crash ('an ever-fixed mark'). To a wandering ship ('bark') it is a guiding star.

In the third section, we see that time takes away the beauty of 'rosy lips and cheeks', but it doesn't take away love. 'Hours

---

1 *The Book of Common Prayer*, the 1552 edition that Shakespeare would have known.

and weeks' go by, but love doesn't alter until the very end of the world ('the edge of doom').

The final couplet suggests that the poet wants us to know how very certain he is and how important he believes it to be. The lines are hammered out in resolute iambs. If it turns out that he is wrong, he will take back every word he has ever put on paper and conclude that nobody in history has ever truly been in love.

I love this poem, which is so simple and so heart-warming. The imagery is not especially original and the thoughts are not complex. But the qualities that make it so compelling are its persistence, restraint and emotional conviction. It uses so many monosyllables. Could there possibly be a hint of doubt? 'Oh no!'

I have heard it read at weddings several times. Every time I hear it I find myself reminded of Paul's great affirmation of the worth of love in 1 Corinthians 13. I can't help wondering whether William had been reading that chapter before he wrote this.

The reason that both have proved timeless is that they deal with straightforward questions that people have always asked, and always will ask, about whether their relationships are of true worth. For a start, Paul addresses the questions that teenage boyfriends and girlfriends WhatsApp their friends about. Is he pushing me faster than I want to go? Why is she always criticizing me? Is he comparing me to past girlfriends? Is she bragging to her friends about things that ought to be private between us? Is he just in it for what he can get out of me? Paul's answers are, respectively: 'Love is patient, love is kind. It does not envy, it does not boast ... it is not self-seeking.'[2]

However, he also addresses the problem of Christians for whom faith has dwindled into a hard-nosed, intolerant dogma that despises any other point of view except a particular kind of orthodoxy – the kind of faith that allows someone to give

---

2 1 Corinthians 13.4, 5 (NIV). The Geneva Bible has: 'Love suffereth long: it is bountiful: love envieth not: love doth not boast itself ... it seeketh not her own thing.'

away every last penny to charity, but cuts off a family member because he or she has made a moral decision that doesn't fit a particular version of the truth. Paul's response is: 'If I have a faith that can move mountains … If I give all I possess to the poor … but do not have love, I gain nothing.'[3]

And Paul speaks directly into the concerns of people who have known each other for a very long time. Don't allow relationships with your parents to be ruined by resentment for things they did years ago that have diminished your life. Find a way through that with love, because 'love keeps no record of wrongs'. Don't create no-go areas with neighbours because of noise or parking or untidiness. Find a way through that with love, because love 'is not easily angered'. Don't find yourself secretly pleased when a friend doesn't get the promotion that would have got them to a better position than you. Find a way through that with love, because love 'does not envy'. Don't give up when your efforts are met with a lack of gratitude of any kind. Find a way through that with love, because love 'always hopes, always perseveres. It never fails'.[4]

That brings us back to Sonnet 116, with the vision it holds out to us of a love that will never come to an end, even in the face of death. It would be possible to dismiss this as idealized and over-romantic. But if you look at it through the lens of Paul's intensely practical reflection on love, it becomes an inspiration not to give up when it is sorely tempting to do so. It's not starry-eyed. Rather, it's about the dogged effort of making love work when the circumstances are far from ideal, when the first rush of romance has given way to the routine of who puts the bins out, when the hair is grey and when you have had your patience tried for the hundredth time.

---

3 1 Corinthians 13.2, 3 (NIV). The Geneva Bible has: 'If I had all faith, so that I could remove mountains … And though I feed the poor with all my goods … and have not love, it profiteth me nothing.'

4 1 Corinthians 13.4, 5, 7, 8 (NIV). The Geneva Bible has: 'It thinketh no evil … it is not provoked to anger … love envieth not … it hopeth all things: it endureth all things. Love doth never fall away.'

Is it impossibly difficult? Of course. Does it risk damage because sometimes you need to say 'enough is enough' in an abusive relationship? Indeed (be careful). Can it make people sentimental when they ought to be realistic? I suppose so. But maybe today, two weeks into Lent, God is prompting you to think about someone in a slightly different way.

Day 14

Shall I compare thee to a summer's day?

Shall I compare thee to a summer's day?
Thou art more lovely and more temperate.
Rough winds do shake the darling buds of May,
And summer's lease hath all too short a date.
Sometime too hot the eye of heaven shines,
And often is his gold complexion dimmed;
And every fair from fair sometime declines,
By chance or nature's changing course untrimmed.
But thy eternal summer shall not fade,
Nor lose possession of that fair thou owest,
Nor shall death brag thou wand'rest in his shade,
When in eternal lines to time thou growest.
So long as men can breathe or eyes can see,
So long lives this, and this gives life to thee.

Sonnet 18

I do not want to be forgotten. There, I've said it! I have no children, I have trodden lightly on the world, but I don't want to be forgotten.

Every one of the first 17 of Shakespeare's sonnets urges the person to whom they are written to have children. The Bible also repeatedly speaks of the blessing of giving birth to the next generation. But in both cases there is an exception and that is where we are looking for heart and hope today.

Shakespeare's sonnets fall into two groups. The first 126 are addressed to a young man – the 'fair youth'. He is handsome, confident and popular. Sometimes the poet is so obsessed with him that he cannot sleep; sometimes he lashes out because his love is unrequited. They are full of homo-erotic charge, often deeply romantic and sometimes they feature sexual innuendo. The second group, numbers 127 to 154, is addressed to a married woman with whom the poet is having an affair – the 'dark lady', so called because of the colour of her hair and skin. She doesn't have the refined intelligence and beauty of the young man. Rather, this is all about adulterous sex – sometimes explicitly so.

The 17 poems that begin the sequence are called 'the procreation sonnets' because of the repeated entreaty to the young man to have children. He is so good-looking, the poet explains, that it would be wicked to deprive the world of the beauty that his children will have.

Sonnet number 1 begins: 'From fairest creatures we desire increase / That thereby beauty's rose might never die.' In other words, the most lovely creatures are expected to have children so that their beauty will be passed on and never die. That is how people will remain unforgotten – their children and grandchildren will be a constant reminder. Sometimes the way William expresses it is frankly bleak: 'But if thou live remembered not to be / Die single and thine image dies with thee' (Sonnet 3).

And then comes the gorgeous poem we are reading today, Sonnet 18, and everything changes. There is another way altogether to be sure that you will not be forgotten.

'Shall I compare thee to a summer's day?' is the most well-known beginning to a Shakespeare poem. He goes on to explain all the ways the young man is better than summer, 'more lovely and more temperate'. Summer can be uncomfortably breezy, especially May. And it always ends too soon – it only has a 'lease', not a permanent residency, and that has 'all too short a date'. The 'eye of heaven' gets too hot, or its sunshine is unpredictably dimmed by clouds. Nothing that is beautiful lasts, because it 'from fair sometime declines' either by an accident of some kind or simply because nature takes its course.

The fair youth is better because he will never diminish in the way summer does. He will never be forgotten because these poetic words describe him and they will still be read 'so long as men can breathe or eyes can see'. Death will be unable to boast about having taken him because he has been immortalized in the words the poet has written: 'Nor shall death brag thou wand'rest in his shade'. With or without children, he will not be forgotten.

It follows the pattern that is typical of the sonnets. The first four lines belong together, with alternate lines rhyming. The way a rhyming structure like this is described is ABAB. The next quatrain is the same – CDCD. Notice how true the rhymes are and how regular the rhythm. Nothing ruffles the quiet progress towards a happy conclusion. The first eight lines are occupied by a single theme – the young man's beauty being greater than the summer. Then there is a development in the following six lines, heralded by 'But'. The technical term for this shift is a volta. Lines 9 to 12 begin the idea that the fair youth is going to be immortal because the poem will outlive him. The rhymes follow the pattern EFEF. And the final couplet (GG) buttons the meaning.

It's easy to understand why this is a favourite sonnet for so many people. Other sonnets have more interesting imagery and more complex structures, but here the accruing features of summer are straightforwardly charming. It is simple and it addresses a longing that is deep within us all. We want to defy time.

The sadness of having no children to maintain your memory and your name is one that reverberates through the Old Testament. In the book of Ruth, Naomi's sons die young and she would have been left alone had it not been for Ruth's loyalty. In her sorrow she wants to change her name to Mara, which means bitterness.[1] Hannah is so distressed at her childlessness that she cannot even put it into words.[2]

This pain was especially acute for the Jews who were captured in the sixth century BC when Jerusalem was overrun by Babylon. Dragged savagely into exile many miles from their

1 Ruth 1.20.
2 1 Samuel 1.13–16.

homeland, they could imagine no future for themselves. The metaphorical childlessness was compounded by the fact that Babylonian conquerors routinely castrated their male captives. The shame was felt not merely because they were unable to have children, but because eunuchs were excluded from God's people and forbidden to worship in the assembly of the Jews.[3] Membership of the community that God had chosen as his own was understood to be based on land and family, and they had lost both.

Into the despair of that generation God spoke words that are absolutely wonderful. They come to us through the prophet Isaiah:

> [Do not] let the Eunuch say, Behold, I am a dry tree.
> For thus saith the Lord unto the Eunuchs that keep my
>   Sabbaths, and choose the thing that pleaseth me, and take
>   hold of my covenant,
> even unto them will I give in mine House and within my
>   walls a place, and a name better than of the sons and of
>   the daughters;
> I will give them an everlasting name, that shall not be put
>   out.[4]

A memorial and a name. Better than sons and daughters. Among the countless blessings that follow a choice to bind yourself to God is this treasure: you will never be forgotten. You will enjoy a spiritual kinship with a Saviour that is more lasting than any physical family.

> Can a woman forget her child, and not have compassion on
>   the son of her womb?
> Though they should forget, yet will I not forget thee.
> Behold, I have graven thee upon the palm of mine hands.[5]

---

3 Deuteronomy 23.1.
4 Isaiah 56.3–5.
5 Isaiah 49.15, 16.

This image of God as a writer comes at the perfect moment on our journey through Shakespeare's work. But in this image, which is also from the book of Isaiah, he doesn't write on parchment; he writes on his very self.

Your name is known to God. Your body and soul, beautiful as a summer's day or battered by nature's changing course, are loved by God. The essence of you is not just written on his hands; it is etched there immovably. In eternal lines to time thou growest.

Enjoy this moment and let your preciousness sink in. You will never be forgotten.

Day 15

Grief fills the room up of my absent child

CONSTANCE: Grief fills the room up of my absent child,
Lies in his bed, walks up and down with me,
Puts on his pretty looks, repeats his words,
Remembers me of all his gracious parts,
Stuffs out his vacant garments with his form;
Then, have I reason to be fond of grief?
Fare you well: had you such a loss as I,
I could give better comfort than you do.
I will not keep this form upon my head,
When there is such disorder in my wit.
O Lord! My boy, my Arthur, my fair son!
My life, my joy, my food, my all the world!
My widow-comfort, and my sorrows' cure!

King John, Act 3, Scene 4

In August 1596, Hamnet died. He was aged 11.

Nobody knows why he died. Nor do we know how Shakespeare, miles away in London, found out about the death of his only son or whether he returned to Stratford-upon-Avon for the funeral. What is known, however, is that about this time he wrote these heart-breaking words about the death of a child.

In *King John*, they are spoken by Constance. Her son Arthur escapes a murder attempt, only to be killed later by falling from a wall as he tries to flee. She enters with her beautiful hair wild and barely able to control her speech. The men around her tell her to get a grip and to tidy herself up. But why should she make her hair orderly ('keep this form upon my head') when her mind ('my wit') is running riot with disorder? Her child has been taken from her. Her joy has been taken from her. She has abandoned herself to grief because that is the only thing left that is hers and cannot be taken from her. 'You are as fond of grief as of your child,' says one of the men, prompting these shattering words.

Arthur is gone, she says, so she is filling all the spaces where he once was with her anguish. His empty bed? It's not empty because it is full of her grief. His 'vacant garments'? They are so full of her grief that you could believe they were being worn. (The clothes! When you have lost someone you love it's always the clothes, isn't it?)

And then that cry of 'Oh Lord!' Is it a sigh or a shriek? That's one of the decisions an actor needs to make when rehearsing the speech. It could be either and it gives way to three lines in which she repeatedly stabs herself with pairs of despairing words.

It's a marvellous speech. It emasculates the men with its depth of feeling. 'You're mad,' they protest. But Constance declares that, faced with what she is enduring, it would be mad not to be mad. She exits and disappears from the play. We later learn that she has died.

A thousand years before Jesus, King David learnt of the death of his son. Absalom was adored by his father, wildly popular and handsome – he too had beautiful hair. But he had ambitions to be king and raised a revolt against David. His army was vanquished and he fled. In a bizarre accident, his hair caught in a tree and he was pulled off his mule. He was stabbed to death by one of David's officers.

David was informed that his army had been victorious. But moments later, the news came that his son had been killed in the rout and it overwhelmed him: 'O my son Absalom, my son, my son Absalom: would God I had died for thee, O Absalom, my son, my son.'[1]

David was urged not to display his true feelings because it would have demoralized his troops, who had suffered their own losses to achieve a victory over his son. So he took a seat in front of them, smothered his sorrow and remained silent. 'Oh my son, my son.' The stabbing!

---

[1] 2 Samuel 18.33.

It's not easy for Christians to grieve. Taught week after week that death is a gateway to joy and glory, it's possible to feel obliged to treat the funeral of someone deeply loved as a celebration. But the truth is that a death is a desperate sadness and it takes a long time to work out your new identity without the company of someone who has been key to the meaning of your life.

Jesus is, of course, absolutely central to finding that meaning. But it is not the Jesus of the empty tomb and eternal joy who is the true source of hope. It is the Jesus who stood near the body of his dead friend Lazarus and cried with the pain of it.[2] That is the reality of the human journey.

And yet! And yet there is something odd about the story of the raising of Lazarus. It is often referred to as the occasion on which Jesus weeps. But if you read it as if you had never encountered it before it seems more like the story in which Jesus doesn't weep.

When Jesus was told that Lazarus was critically ill, he did nothing for two days. There were no tears. When news arrived that Lazarus was dead, Jesus was unmoved – still no tears. And then, four days after his bereavement, surrounded by people saying, 'When it really counted Jesus turned out to be incapable of doing anything,' Jesus wept.

Why then? Why would that moment be the one at which Jesus 'groaned in the spirit' so much that tears flowed?

I can't be sure, but this is what I think. That was the moment when Jesus realized the enormity of what he was going to do. His closest friend was in Paradise. The purposes of life were complete for Lazarus and in heaven he had reached the joy and perfection which is the destiny of humankind. Only Jesus could have known the full wonder of the place at which Lazarus had arrived. And he was about to drag Lazarus back. Back to this earth, where there is grief and pain and uncertainty and loss. I think that's why Jesus wept. Silence was no longer possible.

And silence, in a curious way, leads us back to *King John*. It's a peculiar play. The signing of the Magna Carta, which

---

2 John 11.35.

from the perspective of the twenty-first century seems the most significant event of his reign, doesn't feature in it. Instead, it focuses on war between the King of England and the King of France. Various inconclusive battles are complicated by the Pope, who has excommunicated John, and the English nobles, who keep swapping sides.

The original audiences can't have been gripped by the plot, which unfolds as one unpredictable thing after another. They would have found the resonances with their own age more compelling. Historical monarchs with competing claims to the throne must have made them reflect on Queen Elizabeth and Mary Queen of Scots in their own century. Excommunications, royal death warrants and shipwrecked armies were features of both John's and Elizabeth's reigns.

But the most intriguing thing about the play is its close. It ends with the death of the king, as many of the plays do. John is poisoned by a monk. We are used to the tragic hero of a Shakespeare play making a dying speech that wrings your heart. In *King John*, the nobles are gathered around his deathbed and you sense that the play is building towards that climactic moment. When they have all had their say they turn to John in order for him to pronounce his famous last words … There is a silence. He doesn't get a final speech because he has died while they were burbling on. One of them says, 'You breathe these dead news in as dead an ear.'3

This is writing by a man who is absolutely in control of his art. Shakespeare knows precisely how to make the conventions of drama work. But he has such confidence in his grip on an audience that he also knows how to surprise them by breaking the conventions.

Arthur, Absalom, Lazarus. Constance, David, Jesus. Treading the path that all must tread and yearning for someone to heal the broken-hearted and bind up their wounds. 'Woe is me now: for the Lord hath laid sorrow unto my sorrow: I fainted in my mourning, and I can find no rest.'4

---

3 Act 5, Scene 7.
4 Jeremiah 45.3.

Day 16

My dear Lady Disdain! are you yet living?

BEATRICE: I wonder that you will still be talking, Signior
Benedick: nobody marks you.
BENEDICK: What, my dear Lady Disdain! are you yet living?
BEATRICE: Is it possible disdain should die while she hath
such meet food to feed it as Signior Benedick? Courtesy
itself must convert to disdain, if you come in her presence.
BENEDICK: Then is courtesy a turncoat. But it is certain
I am loved of all ladies, only you excepted: and I would I
could find in my heart that I had not a hard heart; for, truly,
I love none.
BEATRICE: A dear happiness to women: they would else have
been troubled with a pernicious suitor. I thank God and my
cold blood, I am of your humour for that: I had rather hear
my dog bark at a crow than a man swear he loves me.
BENEDICK: God keep your ladyship still in that mind!
so some gentleman or other shall 'scape a predestinate
scratched face.
BEATRICE: Scratching could not make it worse, an 'twere
such a face as yours were.
BENEDICK: Well, you are a rare parrot-teacher.
BEATRICE: A bird of my tongue is better than a beast of yours.
BENEDICK: I would my horse had the speed of your tongue,
and so good a continuer. But keep your way, i' God's name;
I have done.

Much Ado About Nothing, Act 1, Scene 1

It was the second half of the 1590s. Confidently in his stride,
Shakespeare wrote *Much Ado About Nothing*. Beatrice and
Benedick, who have known each other of old, are trying to

outdo each other in a battle of wits to express how much they cannot bear each other's company. Anyone who has ever watched a rom-com in a cinema already knows how that one is going to end.

William was rich. The money didn't come from writing plays. The rate was £6 to £10 – in today's money perhaps £1,000. Rather, it came from owning the company. The Lord Chamberlain's Men were extremely successful, except during years when plague stymied the industry. Shakespeare was a shareholder, along with Richard Burbage (the company's lead actor, for whom he wrote roles such as Richard III and King Lear) and others.

The company played at court more than any other. In December 1594, they were invited to perform in front of Elizabeth I. In March 1595, Shakespeare and two associates were paid £20 for 'two comedies shown before Her Majesty in Christmas last'. We also know that he had a great aversion to paying tax on what he had earned. In 1597, he was found guilty of defaulting on a tax payment of five shillings and it happened again the following year.

Alongside fame went frolics. The diary of a lawyer called John Manningham records that during a revival of *Richard III*, a certain lady became so obsessed with the play that she watched it again and again. She sent a message to Richard Burbage that she would 'entertain' him that night if he came to her rooms dressed as Richard III. William, having overheard the conversation, borrowed the costume and went to visit her an hour before. When a message was brought that Burbage had turned up at the appointed time and was outside the door, 'Shakespeare caused return to be made that William the Conqueror came before Richard III'.

Truth or celebrity gossip? Who knows! But a scandal about who has dallied with whom is also at the heart of *Much Ado About Nothing*.

Beatrice and her cousin Hero live in Messina, Italy. In their grand estate they provide lodgings for a group of soldiers returning victorious from a war. Benedick is one of them and so is his friend Claudio. Claudio immediately falls for Hero. Beatrice and Benedick, both sworn to the single life, take up their sparkling war of words where they had previously left off.

Next morning, the friends of Benedick and Beatrice converse about what we all know – that they are ideally suited for each other and that their bantering is a cover for an affection that neither of them will admit. In two unfailingly comic scenes, first Benedick 'accidentally' overhears his friends discussing how much Beatrice loves him, and then the same happens to Beatrice. Inevitably, they both realize that it's actually true.

Also among the company is Don John. He conspires to ruin the general happiness by deceiving Claudio into believing that Hero is cheating on him. (It's never clear why. He is just bitter and petty. He isn't, to be honest, one of Shakespeare's best villains.) Late that night, Hero's maid has a flirtation with one of Don John's fellow soldiers. Don John has contrived for this to be seen by Claudio and he persuades him that he is actually watching Hero being unfaithful.

Claudio chooses the occasion of his wedding to denounce Hero and declare to the congregation that she has cheated on him. She faints. Beatrice and Benedick scheme with the priest to hide her and put out a message that she has died from the shock. In one of those moments where Shakespeare's genius disrupts a comedy with darkness, Benedick asks Beatrice what she wants him to do to prove his love and she snaps, 'Kill Claudio.'

Hero's rescue comes in the unlikely shape of the village's bumbling team of watchmen, led by the delightfully inept constable Dogberry. They overhear Don John's conspirators bragging about the trick they have played and arrest them. Dogberry manages, after much confusion, to explain to Hero's father what has happened. Claudio is desolate. As a penance he agrees that in place of marrying Hero he will marry, unseen, a young woman who will be brought to him veiled the next day.

I don't think you really need me to tell you how this ends, do you? Suffice to say that it is all very satisfactory and this is my favourite of Shakespeare's plays.

The joy of *Much Ado About Nothing* is that we love being in the company of Beatrice and Benedick, convinced that we know more about their relationship than they do. The volley of conversation that we are looking at today is the first time we see them alone together. It's inventively insulting ('Lady Disdain'). It's funny ('Truly, I love none' ... 'A dear happiness to women'). And they each revel in topping the comment that has gone before ('A bird of my tongue is better than a beast of yours').

Shakespeare has created two characters about whom we really care. Histrionic Benedick, who hides his emotions until he decides he is going to be 'horribly in love' with Beatrice.[1] Feisty Beatrice, who is actually rather vulnerable and attributes it to the fact that 'a star danced, and under it I was born'.[2] Forever observing, forever talking, forever noting. In fact, 'noting' is how Shakespeare would have pronounced 'nothing'. That pun is what there was much ado about.

The New Testament has a great deal to say about talking and noting. What we say and how we say it is important to God. Here it is put very directly: 'Let your speech be gracious always, and powdered with salt, that ye may know how to answer every man.'[3] Gracious, knowing and yet salty is precisely how Shakespeare has made his hero and heroine speak. How are we, with a hundredth of his eloquence, going to do that?

The first step is to note that conversation is changing. During the 16 centuries between the writing of the New Testament and Shakespeare's time, conversation barely changed at all. It required two people to be in the same location looking at each other. With the invention of the telephone, that began to change. It became possible to converse without seeing the subtleties of the other person's expressions. New developments have accelerated and every one of them has increased the possibility that conversation will fail to meet the standards

---

1 Act 2, Scene 3.
2 Act 2, Scene 1.
3 Colossians 4.6.

of the Bible verse. SMS texting made a conversation possible without being aware of either facial reactions or tone of voice. And now social media have taken away the need for us to know the person we are talking to at all. We can say things to someone without recognizing their voice, their face, or even their humanity.

The result is that Twitter can be a place where people shout at and wound strangers without the restraint that physical presence would encourage. Facebook can amplify rumour and ridicule because there is no noting. Where is the graciousness and knowledge or, for that matter, the saltiness?

Christians can, if they choose, model a different way of conversing on social media. They can come to it with the attitude of the proverb that tells us that, 'A word spoken in his place is like apples of gold with pictures of silver.'[4]

It begins with a conscious effort to 'be gracious always', choosing words with care so that people find what we say life-enhancing. It continues with 'knowledge of how to answer every man' and woman by recognizing that they are made in God's image and worthy of an effort to understand them, even if we disagree. And as for being salty? Well, today's hero and heroine were not cloying – they had edgy, witty fun with their banter, but they were never tasteless.

I am always slightly disappointed when Christians announce that they are giving up Twitter for Lent. That platform can sometimes be a hurtful place. The Christian voices there can offer an alternative – encouragement, uplift, challenge, inspiration. If we disappear for 40 days it diminishes the platform. Let's get deeply involved and bring with us apples of gold and pictures of silver.

Lady Disdain has an obstinate and ugly presence on social media. We can be different. #BeMoreBeatrice #BeMoreBenedick

---

4 Proverbs 25.11.

Day 17

What is honour? A word!

PRINCE HARRY: Thou owest God a death. *(Exit.)*
FALSTAFF: 'Tis not due yet. I would be loath to pay Him
before His day. What need I be so forward with Him that
calls not on me? Well, 'tis no matter. Honour pricks me
on. Yea, but how if honour prick me off when I come on?
How then? Can honour set to a leg? No. Or an arm? No.
Or take away the grief of a wound? No. Honour hath no
skill in surgery, then? No. What is honour? A word. What
is in that word 'honour'? What is that 'honour'? Air. A trim
reckoning. Who hath it? He that died o' Wednesday. Doth
he feel it? No. Doth he hear it? No. 'Tis insensible, then?
Yea, to the dead. But will it not live with the living? No.
Why? Detraction will not suffer it. Therefore, I'll none of it.
Honour is a mere scutcheon. And so ends my catechism.

Henry IV Part 1, Act 5, Scene 1

In the Old Testament Apocrypha,[1] a book called Ecclesiasticus
gives a list of people who have achieved honour.

Let us now praise famous men, and our fathers that begat
us. The Lord hath wrought great glory by them through his
great power from the beginning. Such as did bear rule in their
kingdoms, men renowned for their power, giving counsel by
their understanding.

---

[1] The Apocrypha is an appendix to the Old Testament of 14 books
that appear in translations of the Bible used by Roman Catholics, but
not by Protestants. An alternative name for Ecclesiasticus is Sirach.

As well as kings, the list goes on to include musicians, poets, people who gained great wealth, biblical heroes and some who were esteemed in their day but are now forgotten: 'These were honoured in their generations, and were the glory of their times. There be of them that have left a name behind them that their praises might be reported.'[2]

In the culture in which the Old Testament was written, honour was a deeply important concept. The Hebrew word for honour means to give weight to someone – to hold them in such respect that their name endures. Not only should such people be revered, but they are owed attention and obedience. Parents are honoured when their children are respectful. Temple priests are honoured by being given clothes of great distinction to wear. God is honoured by actions that are pleasing to him. For human beings to be honoured is only possible because of the dignity God has bestowed on them by creating them to be only a little lower than angels.[3]

How is a person to live in a way that is recognized as honourable, both in life and in the way he or she is remembered after death? The book of Proverbs has this as one of its themes. It begins with a determination to seek wisdom, that capacity of mind that allows us to understand life from God's perspective. Wisdom is given a voice: 'I love them that love me: and they that seek me early shall find me. Riches and honour are with me: even durable riches and righteousness.'[4] Honour is paired fitly with the pursuit of righteousness and, for those who know the teaching of Jesus, uncomfortably with the pursuit of wealth. Other qualities that pave the path to honour in that book are humility about one's success, resolve to avoid conflict and an abundance of love. However, Proverbs includes a warning that people are inclined to attribute honour to the wrong people. It is not only in the twenty-first century that celebrity is conferred on those who have not really earned

2 Ecclesiasticus 44.1–3, 7–8.
3 Psalm 8.5. The Geneva Bible is even more striking, describing men and women as 'a little lower than God'.
4 Proverbs 8.17, 18.

it: 'As the snow in the summer, and as the rain in the harvest are not meet, so is honour unseemly for a fool.'[5]

So if to honour means to give weight to someone, what kind of rambunctious character would you expect Shakespeare to create in order to scorn and mock honour? He created a 'fat-guts', 'a whoreson round man', a 'huge bombard of sack' – Sir John Falstaff.[6] Not many Shakespeare characters are described in terms of what they look like, but Falstaff is again and again. He himself blames sighs and griefs for inflating him like a balloon. But he likes himself that way. He points out that in the Old Testament, in the dream that Joseph has about years of plenty being succeeded by years of famine, it is scrawny cows that are bad news, not fat ones.[7] What use is it to be held in honour once you are dead when there are jokes to be told and feasts to be scoffed while you are alive? He is drunken, lascivious, corrupt, manipulative and lazy. Yes! He is also the most popular comic character Shakespeare created.

Henry IV Part 1 is about the making of the heroic monarch Henry V. He is a man with two fathers. His true father Henry IV is stern and aloof, tormented by guilt about the murder of Richard II which propelled him to the throne. For him, honour is to be the legitimate ruler of a nation that is thriving in peace. But he can never achieve that because he has to deal with a rebellion by a family of northern noblemen, the Percys, who are aggrieved that Henry will not acknowledge his debt to them. The eldest son of the family has earned the nickname Hotspur because of his ferocity in battle. Hotspur's concept of honour is related to glory on the battlefield and the defence of his integrity when insulted.

But the future Henry V (known as Harry or Hal in the play) has found an alternative father in Falstaff. He is irresistibly drawn to the rollicking life of the robbers and whores who make up Falstaff's gang. And there is without doubt real affection between him and the colossal rogue, which is why the

---

5 Proverbs 26.1.
6 Act 2, Scene 2; Act 2, Scene 5.
7 Act 2, Scene 5, referencing Genesis 41.

audience loves both of them. The dilemma at the heart of the play is which of the two worlds will eventually win Harry's loyalty. Will he be able, as he claims, to cast off dishonour when the time is right and prove himself in battle against the king's enemies?

And what of Falstaff's view of honour? As the play gathers to its climax, all the male characters are preparing for war. Prince Harry has made the momentous decision to join the army of the king and fight Hotspur. Falstaff has followed him into battle, but is determined to turn that to his personal profit. He can't help himself. As he points out, if Adam fell into wrongdoing when the world all around him was perfect, what chance did Falstaff have of staying virtuous when the world around him is full of skulduggery?[8]

In his soliloquy he says that he knows he is going to die, but he has no intention of risking anything that would speed it up. Honour may spur him on, but he's not going to let honour bump him off ('prick me'). Honour is of no use whatever. It can't mend a broken leg. It's not a painkiller. And all the people who have honour are dead ('died o' Wednesday'). They get no enjoyment out of their honour. Sooner or later even their honour will be tarnished because some slanderer will start telling tales ('detraction will not suffer it'). Honour is not a reality but an escutcheon (a painted coat of arms). And that is Falstaff's catechism.

It's interesting that Shakespeare uses the word catechism. It's a statement of what Christians believe laid out, like the speech, as a series of questions and answers. Falstaff's opinion of honour could not possibly be more unlike the description of honour in the Old Testament. However, his character has very surprising origins. Although he is called John Falstaff in the printed edition of the play, in its first performance he was called John Oldcastle. There are jokes still in the play about old castles. The name was changed because there really was a John Oldcastle in the time of Henry IV, two centuries previ-

---

8 Act 3, Scene 3, referencing Genesis 3.

ously, and his descendants were outraged that his honour had been trashed in the play.

Sir John Oldcastle was a profoundly Christian man of impeccable moral character. He was a friend of Prince Harry, but was in the unfortunate position of being a resolute Protestant many years before such a thing existed. He was a Lollard. He wanted the Bible to be available in English, not Latin. He believed that the bread and wine of the eucharist were a way of remembering Jesus, rather than his actual body and blood. He prayed to Jesus, not to saints. He wanted church money to be spent on the poor, not decoration and statues. In fact, he personified the virtues that characterize a person of honour in Proverbs.

The real Henry IV wanted him executed, but it proved impossible because of his close friendship with Prince Harry. When Harry became Henry V, the circumstances changed and he had to take action against Oldcastle because he was destabilizing the Church. He imprisoned him in the Tower of London, but Oldcastle escaped. He was on the run for four years, gathering support for a plot that would overthrow the Catholic Henry V and establish a regency. A huge reward was offered for his capture and he was finally run aground and hanged.

It is entirely unclear what happened in Shakespeare's imagination to turn the honourable Christian Sir John Oldcastle into the 'bolting-hutch of beastliness' that is Falstaff.[9] I would really like to have met Oldcastle and told him how much I admire his integrity and staunch faith. And yet, if I am completely honest, that pales to insignificance compared with how much I would have liked a Friday evening at the Boar's Head Tavern, Eastcheap, in the company of Falstaff. And there lies the enduring popularity of this marvellous play.

How does it end for our hero? We know that Hotspur is defeated and Henry IV is strengthened. But does Prince Harry come good and leave Falstaff when he leaves the battlefield? The series finale is splendidly ambiguous. We're going to need a sequel.

---

9 Act 2, Scene 5.

Day 18

Presume not that I am the thing I was

HENRY V: I know thee not, old man. Fall to thy prayers.
How ill white hairs become a fool and jester!
I have long dreamt of such a kind of man,
So surfeit-swelled, so old, and so profane;
But being awaked, I do despise my dream.
Make less thy body hence, and more thy grace;
Leave gormandizing; know the grave doth gape
For thee thrice wider than for other men –
Reply not to me with a fool-born jest;
Presume not that I am the thing I was,
For God doth know, so shall the world perceive,
That I have turn'd away my former self;
So will I those that kept me company.
When thou dost hear I am as I have been,
Approach me, and thou shalt be as thou wast,
The tutor and the feeder of my riots.
Till then I banish thee, on pain of death,
As I have done the rest of my misleaders,
Not to come near our person by ten mile.
For competence of life I will allow you,
That lack of means enforce you not to evils;
And, as we hear you do reform yourselves,
We will, according to your strengths and qualities,
Give you advancement.

Henry IV Part 2, Act 5, Scene 5

There have only been two sequels that truly match the brilliance of the original. One is *Paddington 2* and the other is the New Testament. *Henry IV Part 2* cannot compete, but it is very funny, extremely affecting, and when the two parts are performed together in one day they comprise my favourite of Shakespeare's plays. It was created because the public wanted more of Falstaff. In fact, they wanted him so much that Shakespeare created another sequel as well. It was called *The Merry Wives of Windsor* and showed Falstaff not in royal company but romping through the bourgeois setting of a quiet town with sex on his brain.

The clamour for sequels by public (and, anecdotally, also royal) demand is an indication of the high regard in which Shakespeare was held by 1598. A book called *Wit's Treasury* survives, written by a theatre-loving vicar called Francis Meres. He comments on the playwrights and poets of the day whom he considers most significant, including Ben Jonson and Christopher Marlowe. But he lavishes praise on 'honey-tongued Shakespeare'. He reveals that a collection of his 'sugared sonnets' was in circulation 'among his private friends'. In praise of the plays, he writes that Shakespeare is 'the most passionate [writer to] bemoan the perplexities of love'. He lists all the 'most excellent' plays written by that date as either comedies or tragedies, which helps scholars date them. He puts *Henry IV* among the tragedies.

With his stock rising, William was able to invest in property. Back home, he purchased New Place. It was the second largest house in Stratford-upon-Avon. Its grounds had two barns and an orchard. Its site and garden can still be visited on Chapel Street. However, the house is no longer standing because in 1756 the vicar who lived there, Francis Gastrell, grew so fed up with visitors knocking on his door asking to see Shakespeare's residence that he had it knocked down. Thus did two clergymen secure their contrasting reputations in history as spear-carriers in the drama of Shakespeare's life.

In *Henry IV Part 2*, rebel leaders who have survived their defeat at the end of *Part 1* regroup and consider how to reverse the tide of the civil war. The king has aged prematurely under the toll of the war and his worries over his son Prince Harry's waywardness. Falstaff, as jovial as ever, is making the most of the attention he attracted because of the fake news that it was he who killed Hotspur and is voraciously converting the money that came with it into beer and prostitutes. Harry rejoins his old partners-in-crime in the Boar's Head Tavern. There is teasing, disguise and tomfoolery, but his fun with Falstaff seems to have an unkind edge to it. Harry knows change is on its way.

Falstaff tours the countryside conscripting young men for the inevitable battles, but anyone who can afford a bribe is excused. This means that he gathers an army that can barely stand, let along fight. In a touching and funny scene he reminiscences with Justice Shallow, with whom he grew up, and they lament the passing of the years. Gone are the days when they could stay up until the middle of the night and only girls and dinner mattered: 'We have heard the chimes at midnight, Master Shallow … That we have; that we have.'[1]

Harry meets his father, now very frail, and the king castigates him. In a powerful scene, the prince thinks his father is dead and puts on the crown. But he is actually in an enfeebled sleep and comes to the worst conclusions about his son when he wakes. Harry makes an eloquent, repentant speech and the two are reconciled. When Henry IV dies, Harry tells the Lord Chief Justice that he now views him as his father.

The rebels are crushed and Harry steps up to be crowned Henry V. Crowds gather in the street to acclaim him and among them are Falstaff and his ne'er-do-wells, anticipating the lucrative high office that they believe is their destiny. The new king catches sight of Falstaff and stops. And then today's speech.

'I know thee not, old man.' Someone with white hair has reached the time of life when he should be praying, not fooling and jesting. Harry says that he recognizes Falstaff from a dream he once had. But he has woken up and, 'I do despise my dream.' It is time for someone like the fat knight to lose weight and gain dignity. Harry has made his peace with God and changed: 'Presume not that I am the thing I was.'

---

1 Act 3, Scene 2.

He creates an exclusion order which means that Falstaff cannot come within ten miles of him. He gives him a small allowance which means that he will not be destitute ('for competence of life') and will be able to live without resorting to crime. And he holds out the hope that Falstaff will reform himself, which might mean he considers the possibility of more ('give you advancement'). And then he is gone, leaving Falstaff broken with embarrassment among his friends and coping with it by denial.

The speech is devastating. It is delivered in iambic pentameters – measured, stately. The contrast with the tumbling prose of yesterday's speech by Falstaff could not be greater. It is an unhurried condemnation. Phrases are inverted to give a sense of loftiness ('reply not ... presume not' instead of 'do not presume'). And it takes 25 lines to say what could be said in two so that the pain is intensified.

Henry V has repented of his past life. As always in life, repentance requires change. He chooses to demonstrate that change by cutting off any possibility of being tempted back into his old life. But he delivers his judgement and calls others to repent with an authority that, as far as the audience is concerned, he has not yet earned. It is cruel. It is the fiery demand for repentance that we associate with Elijah or John the Baptist. But it doesn't come with the integrity of an austere life in the desert; it comes from the luxury of an inherited palace.

We know that, were their destinies somehow switched, Falstaff would not do this to his old friend. The reason we know it comes from their very first scene together, some five hours of stage time previously. Falstaff had heard one of the king's council berating the delinquent Harry in public, just as the new king is doing to him now: 'An old lord of the council rated me the other day in the street about you, sir, but I marked him not; and yet he talked very wisely, but I regarded him not.' At the time Harry replied: 'Thou didst well; for wisdom cries out in the streets, and no man regards it.'[2]

---

2 *Henry IV Part 1*, Act 1, Scene 2.

That's a direct quotation from the Bible. It comes from Proverbs. Harry uses it to justify the fact that he is not listening to anyone who is pleading with him to behave. 'Wisdom cries out in the street; in the squares she raises her voice: ... How long will scoffers delight in their scoffing and fools hate knowledge? ... I have stretched out my hand and no one heeded.'[3] We are back in the company of Wisdom, who featured in yesterday's reflection. She is the personification of a way of thinking that sees the world through godly eyes. She too calls people to repent and she threatens to do the very thing that King Henry is doing to Falstaff: 'I also will laugh at your calamity; I will mock when panic strikes you, when panic strikes you like a storm.'[4]

No matter what our human instincts are to find satisfaction in people suffering misfortune when that is what they deserve, God is a God who never leaves men and women without a way back. With repentance comes forgiveness. Always!

Proverbs continues: 'My child, if you will accept my words ... then you will understand righteousness and justice and equity, every good path; for wisdom will come into your heart.'[5] This is the relentlessly gracious nature of God, never ceasing in his pursuit of a human heart. Here in the marrow of Lent he is raising his voice, he is stretching out his hand.

There is a hint of this in Henry's speech too, for he offers Falstaff the possibility of a way back 'as we hear you do reform yourselves'. It keeps my hopes alive, because I am inexplicably under the spell of that fatberg of comical vice. But I have a doleful feeling that this humiliation will be too much for him. We'll find out tomorrow.

---

3 Proverbs 1.20, 22, 24.
4 Proverbs 1.26, 27.
5 Proverbs 2.1, 9, 10.

Day 19

We few, we happy few, we band of brothers

HENRY V: He which hath no stomach to this fight,
Let him depart; his passport shall be made
And crowns for convoy put into his purse:
We would not die in that man's company
That fears his fellowship to die with us.
This day is called the feast of Crispian:
He that outlives this day, and comes safe home,
Will stand a tip-toe when the day is named,
And rouse him at the name of Crispian.
He that shall live this day, and see old age,
Will yearly on the vigil feast his neighbours,
And say 'Tomorrow is Saint Crispian.'
Then will he strip his sleeve and show his scars.
And say 'These wounds I had on Crispin's day.' ...
We few, we happy few, we band of brothers;
For he today that sheds his blood with me
Shall be my brother; be he ne'er so vile,
This day shall gentle his condition:
And gentlemen in England now a-bed
Shall think themselves accursed they were not here,
And hold their manhoods cheap whiles any speaks
That fought with us upon Saint Crispin's day.

Henry V, Act 4, Scene 3

These are the rousing words of a political leader who believes unflinchingly that he has God on his side.

The words were first spoken in 1599 from the stage of the brand new Globe Theatre. We can be sure of that because there is a prologue to *Henry V* which asks the audience to imagine thousands of soldiers fighting on the open fields of Agincourt, in Northern France, when all we can see is a handful of actors on a small stage in London: 'May we cram / Within this wooden O the very casques [helmets] / That did affright the air at Agincourt?' The 'wooden O' is the distinctive shape of the Globe Theatre, circling the stage with a pit for a standing audience and three levels of bench seating.

The lease on the land on which the Lord Chamberlain's Men formerly had their theatre expired in 1598. After months of stalled negotiations, during a bitterly cold winter, the actors dismantled the building and carried it piece by piece across the frozen River Thames. They rebuilt it in Southwark as a dedicated venue for plays – no bear-baiting or blood sports. It stood there for 13 years until it burned down during a performance. A replica of the Globe Theatre stands on the banks of the Thames today. It's not on the original site, but is close to it.

That wooden O hosted the premieres of some of the most famous plays ever written and *Henry V* is among them. It is set in the early fifteenth century and Shakespeare researched it, as he did with all his history plays, using a 1577 book by Raphael Holinshed called the *Chronicles of England, Scotland and Ireland*. The wild, undisciplined Harry whom we met in *Henry IV Parts 1 and 2* is now approaching 30 and is transforming himself into Henry V, one of the great warrior-kings of England.

Henry has a claim to lands in the north of France, based on distant ancestry and a selective interpretation of some ancient laws. He is triggered by an insult from the Dauphin (the young French prince) who sends him a gift of a crate of tennis balls to remind everyone of his sportive past. Incensed, Henry vows to create 'many a thousand widows' in France and invokes God as his inspiration: 'This lies all within the will of God / To whom I do appeal, and in whose name / Tell you the Dauphin I am coming on / To venge me.'[1]

In the Boar's Head Tavern, the lowlifes who were once his brothers-in-crime prepare for war again. From the previous

---

1 Act 1, Scene 2.

plays we welcome back Bardolph, Pistol and Nym but not Falstaff, whose death is described comically but fondly. He was, perhaps, such a walloping character that he would have unbalanced a play in which heroism is all-important.

The English troops advance through France and win victories against the odds. Outside Harfleur, Henry delivers an impassioned speech, urging his men to charge recklessly through the breach (the crack that has been battered in the city's walls), abandoning their humanity and imagining themselves to be tigers: 'Once more into the breach, dear friends, once more ... Stiffen the sinews, summon up the blood / Disguise fair nature with hard-favoured rage.' The speech ends with Henry roaring that if England is victorious, God is victorious: 'Cry God for Harry, England and St George!'[2] Bardolph is caught looting, and Henry orders him hanged without a flicker of regret.

The war comes to a climax at the Battle of Agincourt. The night before, Henry disguises himself so that he can walk among his soldiers and find out what they think of him and of the war they are fighting. He discovers that they question his motives and his courage. Alone, he tells the audience of the loneliness of leadership. He loves being king because of the clothes and ceremony, but actually he would rather be a slave who can sleep at night without worrying about the safety of an entire country. He prays to God that he will forget for 24 hours the fact that his father came to the throne by murdering Richard II. He asks God to give his troops courage and that they will never discover how outnumbered they are.

And so to today's dazzling speech. As the day of the battle dawns, Henry tells anyone who isn't yearning to fight to leave. He will give them a safe passage home. The feast day of St Crispin and St Crispinian is 25 October. They were twin brothers who fled Rome at the end of the third century when Christians were facing persecution. They fetched up in the north of France, where they preached Christianity by day and supported themselves by making shoes by night until their martyrdom.

---

2 Act 3, Scene 1.

This is a speech that unashamedly wills men to fight. It appeals to the esteem in which they will be held by those who, in years to come, will see their scars and hear their story. It appeals to the notion of the triumph of the underdog ('we few, we happy few' – the English were outnumbered two to one, or if you believe Shakespeare, five to one). And it appeals to the spurious sentiment that, side by side on the battlefield, those of very different standing are equal ('he that sheds his blood with me shall be my brother').

The English prevail and a peace treaty involves the marriage between Henry and Catherine, the daughter of the French king. The speech suggests Henry is the perfect leader – courageous, inspirational and yet modest. But the way Shakespeare presents him in the rest of the play is more compromised. He sentences old friends to death in the same breath as extolling mercy. He never acknowledges responsibility for the carnage he has initiated, 'mowing like grass your fresh-fair virgins and your flowering infants'.[3] He has invaded a non-aggressive country and slaughtered its citizens in the belief that God is telling him to do so.

The play never settles on a consistent view of warfare. This means that productions through the centuries have allowed audiences to reflect on their own times in different ways. Filmed during the Second World War, it seemed like a patriotic rally.[4] Filmed again during the Soviet-Afghan War, the horror was relentless.[5] Staged in London during the Iraq War, it was seething with cynicism.[6]

In Shakespeare's own time, the glorification of battle must have seemed straightforwardly relevant to England's military ventures in Spain. Eleven years before the play was first performed, Elizabeth I, with 'the body of a weak, feeble woman, but ... the heart and stomach of a king', had rallied her troops

---

3 Act 3, Scene 3.
4 Directed by and starring Laurence Olivier, 1944.
5 Directed by and starring Kenneth Branagh, 1989.
6 Royal National Theatre, directed by Nicholas Hytner and starring Adrian Lester, 2003.

as the Spanish Armada approached by enlisting God on the side of the English: 'We shall shortly have a famous victory over these enemies of my God, of my kingdom, and of my people.'[7] The Armada was defeated because the direction of the wind changed, which was universally attributed to God's intervention in the English cause.

In the heat of the Second World War, Winston Churchill repeatedly invoked God when he addressed the nation. He loved this speech, which is why he referred to the airmen who fought the Battle of Britain as 'the Few'. These are his words at the start of the Blitz: 'It is with devout but sure confidence that I say: Let God defend the right.'[8] Adolf Hitler shared Churchill's love of Shakespeare and sanctioned a radio broadcast of *The Merchant of Venice* immediately after Kristallnacht. He also was eager to recruit God to his cause: 'We are all proud that, through God's powerful aid, we have become once more true Germans ... Who says I am not under the special protection of God?'[9]

We need to look to Abraham Lincoln for sense. God cannot be both for and against the same thing, he declared. '[Opposing sides] read the same Bible and pray to the same God, and each invokes his aid against the other. The prayers of both could not be answered, and those of neither has been answered fully. The Almighty has his own purposes.'[10] And yes, he too cherished Shakespeare and had the Complete Works on his desk in the White House throughout his presidency.

Enough insistence that God must be on our side. A more pertinent question for this season of Lent is whether we have it within us to change and enlist ourselves on God's side. And that is something that we will consider tomorrow.

---

7 The speech to the troops at Tilbury, Essex, 9 August 1588.
8 BBC radio broadcast, 11 September 1940.
9 Speech to the Reichstag, 23 March 1933.
10 Address during the second inauguration, 4 March 1865.

Day 20

All the world's a stage

JACQUES: All the world's a stage,
And all the men and women merely players;
They have their exits and their entrances;
And one man in his time plays many parts,
His acts being seven ages. At first the infant,
Mewling and puking in the nurse's arms;
Then the whining school-boy, with his satchel
And shining morning face, creeping like snail
Unwillingly to school. And then the lover,
Sighing like furnace, with a woeful ballad
Made to his mistress' eyebrow. Then a soldier,
Full of strange oaths, and bearded like the pard,
Jealous in honour, sudden and quick in quarrel,
Seeking the bubble reputation
Even in the cannon's mouth. And then the justice,
In fair round belly with good capon lined,
With eyes severe and beard of formal cut,
Full of wise saws and modern instances;
And so he plays his part. The sixth age shifts
Into the lean and slippered pantaloon,
With spectacles on nose and pouch on side,
His youthful hose, well saved, a world too wide
For his shrunk shank; and his big manly voice,
Turning again toward childish treble, pipes
And whistles in his sound. Last scene of all,
That ends this strange eventful history,
Is second childishness and mere oblivion;
Sans teeth, sans eyes, sans taste, sans everything.

As You Like It, Act 2, Scene 7

As You Like It is about four ways of becoming a loving bride and groom. There is a couple who find the way there by unconventional but romantic wooing. There is a couple who arrive by overcoming differences and proving that change is possible. There is a third couple who decide that, although the circumstances aren't perfect, they will give it a go and hope for the best. And there is a couple who are so shamelessly horny that scenes accelerate to their end because they can't wait to get off stage and rip their pants off.

None of them are judged. All of them affirm life and love. But the play is not schematically happy-ever-after either, because it also features a miserable old codger who won't join the carnival at the end, but stays single and awkward. That's realistic. We all know people like that. And how does Shakespeare punish him? He doesn't. Instead he makes us love him too by giving him the best speech in the play.

'All the world's a stage.' Shakespeare didn't coin the phrase. The poet Juvenal said something similar at about the time the Gospel of John was being written. In Latin, it was the motto of the Globe Theatre and was written on a crest above the entrance. But it had never been used in the melancholy way that Jacques does, suggesting that life can be as fleeting as an actor's appearance in a play – eye-catching in his many changes of costume but then gone and forgotten.

He pictures seven stages of a man's life. A vomiting baby, a reluctant schoolboy, a preposterous lover, a contentious soldier ('pard' is a leopard), an earnest citizen, a doddering old fogey and a decrepit ancient ('sans teeth' means toothless).

This is a very cynical view of the worth of a human. However, it is rescued from being depressing because it is so witty and memorable. And Shakespeare immediately goes on to tell us that although Jacques is entertaining, he is wrong. On to the stage comes an old man, Adam, who has given a lifetime of loyalty and service and is funding with his life savings the down-on-his-luck master who is now carrying him. They both get fed and cared for. It is the best of humanity.

The Bible, in life-affirming contrast to Jacques, speaks of a God who carries human beings with extraordinary love through every stage of their life from birth to death. More than that – from the womb to eternity. These are the words Isaiah attributes to God about the Jewish people, and Christians hear in them a comfort that speaks to their own deepest need:

'Ye are born of me from the womb,
and brought up of me from the birth.
Therefore unto old age I ... will bear you
until the hoary hairs:
I have made you: I will also bear you,
and I will carry you, and I will deliver you.'[1]

The Bible offers seven altogether different pictures of the stages of life. As babies we are introduced to the daughters of Job – Jemimah, Keziah and Keren-Happuch. Job found them so beautiful that they were a blessing to his life after years of loss and suffering.[2]

In the place of a 'whining schoolboy' we meet young Miriam, the sister of the endangered Moses, who was so resourceful beyond her years at the time of his birth that she made it possible for him to be nursed by his mother but raised in a palace.[3]

Relentlessly positive about expressions of love, the Bible outclasses the goofiness of a ballad about an eyebrow by acquainting us with Mary, who made a place for herself in history by weeping for the love of Jesus as she poured perfume on his feet.[4]

The Christian faith has always had a more nuanced approach to being a soldier. In the decades after the resurrection of Jesus, Christians were largely pacifist and subsequently the Emperor Diocletian purged his army of them. However, the Roman army continued to include many Christians and

---

1 Isaiah 46.3, 4.
2 Job 42.14.
3 Exodus 2.1–10.
4 John 12.1–8.

it was their presence that was one of the factors that led to Constantine becoming a believer in the fourth century. For an attitude to military service that was not about the cursing and aggrandizement described in the speech above, we might return to Miriam, who grew up to be regarded as a prophet. After the defeat of the enemy army, she sang of thanksgiving and righteousness: 'The Lord is my strength and praise, and he is become my salvation.'[5]

Alternatively, I could have singled out Deborah, the soldier who led the Hebrew people 12 centuries before Jesus. However, she is better suited to stand as an example of a judge. Unlike Jacques' justice who has a 'fair round belly' (presumably having converted the bribes he has taken into chicken dinners), her court was so respected for the wisdom she showed in settling disputes that its location was named after her – the Palm of Deborah.[6]

God's insistence on the dignity of the human condition persists into old age and is not reduced in any way by the frailty of a person's body. The Bible has no pantaloon with 'shrunk shank' (shrivelled legs) but instead has Elizabeth, the mother of John the Baptist. She showed advanced years to be a state in which, filled with the Holy Spirit, it was possible to discern things that others had not discovered. Opening her home to Mary, pregnant with Jesus, she recognized that she was in the presence of the Saviour.[7]

Even older is Anna – 84, widowed for many decades, and devoted to prayer. Far from being 'sans everything', she had the whole shebang. Meeting the infant Jesus, she bubbled with thanksgiving and wisdom.[8]

Fortunately, the moral heart of *As You Like It* is not found in Jacques, but in a woman called Rosalind. It is her ability to teach others to think and feel and love better than they previously had that heals the bitterness with which the play begins.

---

5 Exodus 15.2.
6 Judges 4.4–5.
7 Luke 1.39–45.
8 Luke 2.36–38.

Rosalind's father Duke Senior has been usurped and exiled by his brother Duke Frederick. Senior has fled with his courtiers to live, Robin Hood-like, in the Forest of Arden and he loves the simplicity he has found there. A nobleman called Orlando is persecuted by his selfish brother Oliver. Both Rosalind and Orlando are banished from Frederick's court, but not before they have met each other and fallen immediately in love.

Orlando escapes to the forest, taking with him his old and faithful servant Adam. There he finds kindness with Duke Senior's band, settles and writes ludicrous romantic poems about Rosalind which he posts on the trees. Rosalind also flees to the forest. However, she disguises herself as a man and takes with her her closest friend, Celia, who is also in disguise.

The lovesick Orlando meets Rosalind and is immediately attracted to her, but because of her disguise thinks she is a boy called Ganymede. He confesses to him/her that he is overwhelmed by his amorous feelings for a girl. Ganymede claims to be an expert in curing people of such emotions and will do so for Orlando if he pretends to woo Ganymede as if he were Rosalind. He does.

On Shakespeare's original stage, all female characters were played by young men. So here we have a boy actor playing the part of a girl, who is disguised as a boy and being courted by a man who is pretending that he is a girl. This not only produces some extremely funny and tender moments, it also allows Shakespeare to comment on gender with a surprisingly modern eye. Teaching the man she secretly loves that a woman's wisdom is unstoppable, Rosalind says: 'Make [lock] the doors upon a woman's wit, and it will out at the casement; shut that, and 'twill out at the keyhole; stop that, 'twill fly with the smoke out at the chimney.'[9]

Orlando is not the only one who changes in the forest. His brother Oliver has pursued him there under orders from Duke Frederick, but he encounters a lioness. By a stroke of good fortune, Orlando stumbles upon them and saves Oliver's life.

---

9 Act 4, Scene 1.

The undeserved generosity prompts Oliver to vow to live a better life. This repentance makes him extremely attractive to the disguised Celia and he falls in love with her, thinking her to be a humble shepherdess.

The capacity for human beings to change becomes even more evident. Duke Frederick himself ventures into the forest with evil intent. But his malice is transformed when he becomes the subject of the only explicit Christian conversion in any of the plays. On his journey he meets an elderly monk, with whom he has a long conversation about the ways of God. He is so moved that he comes to faith, restores the dukedom to his brother Senior and goes to live in a monastery. (Abrupt and unconvincing, yes, but let's enjoy the moment!)

However, the play belongs to Rosalind. She is clever, independent and kind and at the same time as understanding the foolishness of romance she is giddy with the happiness of being in love. When the company leaves the forest to return to the city, everyone who has met her has changed for the better. As the subplots telling the stories of the other lovers drop into place, she succeeds in orchestrating four weddings in the play's closing scene. That includes her own, which is very much as we like it, and the reason why this is my favourite of Shakespeare's plays.

Day 21

That time of year thou mayst in me behold

That time of year thou mayst in me behold
When yellow leaves, or none, or few, do hang
Upon those boughs which shake against the cold,
Bare ruined choirs, where late the sweet birds sang.
In me thou seest the twilight of such day
As after sunset fadeth in the west,
Which by and by black night doth take away,
Death's second self, that seals up all in rest.
In me thou seest the glowing of such fire
That on the ashes of his youth doth lie,
As the death-bed whereon it must expire
Consumed with that which it was nourished by.
   This thou perceivest, which makes thy love more strong,
   To love that well which thou must leave ere long.

Sonnet 73

As You Like It, which we explored yesterday, has dozens of allusions to the Bible. There is a reference to the Parable of the Prodigal Son within the first minute. When the characters escape from the violence and threat of the court, they find their way to the Forest of Arden which, as well as being the name of William's mother, sounds like an amalgam of Garden and Eden. When they encounter the banished duke, he makes it plain that they have found their way to a sort of paradise: 'Here we feel not the penalty of Adam.'[1] They find it to be true. They don't get punished there, but it's a place of healing where love can break through.

---

1 Act 2, Scene 1.

When all is forgiven and the lovers are together, Hymen, the Greek God of weddings, appears to give his blessing. Not the Christian God? No! But what Hymen says is this: 'Then is there mirth in heaven when earthly things made even are atoned together.'[2] That is gratifyingly similar to what Jesus says at the end of the Parable of the Lost Sheep: 'Joy shall be in heaven for one sinner that converteth.'[3]

However, Shakespeare never walks to the front of the stage and gives us the Christian Good News. Whatever his deepest beliefs were, he kept them to himself. Why? One theory is that he was secretly a Catholic, which would have made his company's relationship with Queen Elizabeth awkward. His daughter Susanna is recorded as paying fines for not going to church. Elizabeth I had a lucrative system which allowed Catholics to pay a fine instead of going to a Protestant church. As long as they were discreet, they didn't end up tried for treason and the queen had a money-spinner which was useful in funding the navy when the Spanish Armada threatened.

Maybe the caution over religion was a response to the rise of Puritanism. Puritan Christians hated the theatres and succeeded in having them closed down about 30 years after William's death. They thought theatres were hotbeds of profanity, smut and sexual depravity. Well ... in all honesty, they had a point.

There was a popular joke at the time about a man who allowed his wife to go to the theatre one afternoon. He was worried about security, so he told her to wear her purse deep inside several layers of skirts. When she got home she found she'd been robbed.

'That's ridiculous,' he said. 'Surely you noticed the man's hand reaching there.'

'Of course I did,' said the wife. 'But it never occurred to me that it was the money he was after.'

There was nothing to stop Shakespeare writing something explicit about the nature of Christian salvation. His fellow playwright Christopher Marlowe was born in the same year

---

2 Act 5, Scene 4.
3 Luke 15.7.

and was insistently atheist. However, at the end of his play *Doctor Faustus*, he has a theological statement more specific than anything Shakespeare wrote: 'See, see where Christ's blood streams in the firmament! One drop would save my soul, half a drop.'[4]

Something subtler happens in Shakespeare's plays. People explore the great unknowable issues of life. When they do, nothing goes unquestioned. So in each century, new interpretations make it seem as though they were written to examine today's beliefs, hopes and anxieties. The suggestion that there is a good and gracious God is assumed, mocked, interrogated or cherished by various characters in different plays. For ageing Adam in *As You Like It*, quoting Jesus, it is the hope that sustains him in infirmity: 'He that doth the ravens feed, / Yea, providently caters for the sparrow, / Be comfort to my age!'[5]

It's old age that is the subject of Sonnet 73. The Puritans would not have appreciated this poem either. They wanted poetry to be free from metaphors and verbal flourishes and to focus on biblical subjects. This gorgeous sonnet is rich in everything that riled them.

The first four lines offer a metaphor about a turning year. The poet pictures himself as a tree during those late autumn days when the final colour-drained leaves are hanging on the branches. The birds have flown and their song is gone. The bare boughs remind him of the arches of a ruined abbey when the music the choir once made is just a memory. In the fourth line Shakespeare interrupts the pattern of iambs by adding an extra stress on the first word – bare. (The technical term for two stressed syllables in a row is a spondee.) The result is that three stark adjectives are thumped out in a row – cold, bare, ruined. The desolation is enough to make you shiver. That is his view of old age.

The second quatrain offers a metaphor about a turning day. Dusk is giving way to darkness. Night is described as death's

---

4 *Doctor Faustus*, Scene 13.
5 Act 2, Scene 3, referencing Luke 12.6, 24.

twin – its 'second self'. Light, like life itself, is slowly being extinguished as age increases.

The third quatrain consists of a metaphor about a final ending. The year and the day will return in a cycle, but ultimately there will come a moment when time runs out. The poet in old age is like the glowing remnant of a fire. It rests on the ashes of the logs that once enabled it to burn, just as a person at the end of his life still contains the traces of the youth that once sustained him. The burning that gave the fire life is also responsible for its death ('consumed with that which it was nourished by').

After 12 such sombre lines, the final couplet needs to deliver a profound conclusion. If all this is true, it declares, the only possible response is to love more deeply. Love what? There are two ways of reading it. It could be that the young man should love the poet more passionately because the day will come when he no longer has him. Or it could be that all of us should love the reality of being alive more intensely because one day it will come to an end.

That was the moment at which, if he had chosen to do so, Shakespeare could have hinted at the Christian hope of eternity. He didn't. At this juncture he gave away nothing about his beliefs beyond affirming in a most beautiful way that love is all.

In the New Testament, Paul's prose was equally able to rise to lyrical beauty. Here he is describing the frailty of a human body, but with an altogether more uplifting attitude: 'We are afflicted on every side, yet are we not in distress: we are in doubt, but yet we despair not. We are persecuted, but not forsaken: cast down, but we perish not.'[6]

Paul encourages us to glimpse eternity whenever we are feeling old. He does so with an extraordinary suggestion about the impact of Jesus' death and resurrection. While our outer, physical bodies are growing gradually older, our inner, spiritual lives are growing younger by the day. It defies all logic, but

---

6 2 Corinthians 4.8, 9.

here it is: 'Therefore we faint not, but though our outward man perish, yet the inward man is renewed daily.'[7]

A progressively younger inner life! One day, when all the aches and infirmities catch up with us and we die, our spiritual selves will have worked their way back to day one. And then to zero. And then we will be born again into God's presence, fresh and perfect and full of potential.

What we observe is the year ending, the day ending, the fire going out. Every word of Sonnet 73 is true. But God invites us to see more. How can we do that when the evidence is so compelling? Paul has a proposal: 'Look not on the things which are seen but on the things which are not seen, for the things which are seen are temporal: but the things which are not seen are eternal.'[8]

Because of God's great love for humankind, weakness is part of the preparation for being forever strong. So yes, William, it is indeed all about love. Struggle on. Keep your eyes on your true destination. Grow younger and younger until you are ready for God to pick you up in his arms.

---

7 2 Corinthians 4.16.
8 2 Corinthians 4.18.

Day 22

Like as the waves make towards the pebbled shore

Like as the waves make towards the pebbled shore,
So do our minutes hasten to their end,
Each changing place with that which goes before,
In sequent toil all forwards do contend.
Nativity, once in the main of light,
Crawls to maturity, wherewith being crowned,
Crooked eclipses 'gainst his glory fight,
And time that gave doth now his gift confound.
Time doth transfix the flourish set on youth
And delves the parallels in beauty's brow;
Feeds on the rarities of nature's truth,
And nothing stands but for his scythe to mow.
    And yet to times in hope my verse shall stand,
    Praising thy worth, despite his cruel hand.

Sonnet 60

Time has been kind to William. He predicted it would be. He declared that 'my verse shall stand' despite the cruelty of passing time. His talent is not just spoken of in acclaim, but in awe.

There are some who rate the language, characterization and insight so highly that they contend the son of a glove-maker from a provincial town could not possibly have risen to such literary magnificence. Despite the absence of any credible evidence, they construct arguments why other writers should be considered as the author of the plays and sonnets. Contenders include the essayist and scientist Francis Bacon and the much-travelled theatre-lover, Edward de Vere, the Earl of Essex.

It must be conceded, though, that not everything Shakespeare wrote is flawless. Pretty much every play has a couple of lines that are so obscure that no one seems to know their meaning. His plots can be tortuous, relying on extraordinary coincidences or involving characters who disappear without explanation. There are anachronisms and liberties with historical facts. And the length – ye gods, the length! He can be so much in love with his own language that speeches occupy far more words than the situation warrants. For almost every production today, a director creates a new version which makes the play easier for an audience to appreciate.

He had a reputation in his day for writing at pace, which may account for some of this. The first edition of his collected plays, the *First Folio*, was published in 1623, seven years after his death. In the introduction, his publishers commented on his speed: 'His mind and hand went together.' They also mentioned that his manuscripts were very clean, with few crossings out: 'What he thought he uttered with that easiness that we have scarce received from him a blot in his papers.' His fellow playwright and great rival Ben Jonson responded in exasperation: 'Would he had blotted a thousand.'

Some of the problems that make it difficult for us to fully enjoy the plays are accounted for by the age in which he lived. *The Taming of the Shrew*, for instance, is a comedy about how a feisty, opinionated young woman is overlooked as a marriage partner because of the attention paid to her demure and beautiful sister. A quirky suitor, who may be more interested in the dowry than the woman, succeeds in breaking her by depriving her of food and sleep until she dwindles into the kind of subservient wife she is expected to be. Cue happy ending!

It was probably Shakespeare's first play and it is difficult to read it without cringing. It's infused with the sentiments of its day. Shakespeare, who so often had insights that seem ahead of his time, cannot be blamed for having lived in the sixteenth century. Productions today only succeed if they reframe the plot in an ironic context that shows Katherine, the 'shrew', to be cannier than anyone supposes, going along with the abuse to achieve her own ends. In those circumstances, watching it can still be a rollicking pleasure. However, none of its speeches warrants a day of its own this Lent. It is also filthy, but that's not the reason.

Time has, notwithstanding, been kind to William. It is, as Sonnet 60 reflects, as unremitting as the waves on a beach. Each minute takes the place of the one that went before. You cannot avoid the fact that one day those minutes will come to an end because it is 'all forwards'.

The second quatrain tells the story of a human life as if it were the sun. It has a 'nativity'. In its youth it rises to shine over the ocean ('the main of light'). At noon it is 'crowned' with midlife maturity. But then 'crooked eclipses' begin to take away its glory. Time destroys its own gift.

It will puncture ('transfix') the beauty that goes with youth. It will scrape wrinkles on the loveliest of foreheads ('delve the parallels'). There is nothing that time will not devour – like a harvester scything through wheat, it will cut everything down.

What hope is there then? The closing couplet delights in two things that will outwit time. Poetry will survive ('my verse will stand'). And the worth of the man the poet is addressing will survive, because generations to come will read of him.

The sense that time is moving constantly forward is very significant in Jewish and Christian thought. In ancient Greek thinking the concept was different – the ebb and flow of tides and the cycle of seasons led them to believe that time was cyclical. The sense that processes repeat endlessly gave them a fatalistic view of destiny. Christians have a contrasting view and they are given hope by that.

Psalm 90 uses imagery about the impact of time on a human in a similar way to Sonnet 60, but the metaphor is about grass rather than the sun: 'In the morning it flourisheth and groweth, but in the evening it is cut down and withereth.'[1] No wonder humans are constrained and sometimes dismayed by the shortness of life.

---

1 Psalm 90.5, 6.

God is eternal and time is part of his creation. It is impossible for us wholly to grasp an existence that is outside time. All we know are the days and the years. But God has made it possible to experience a yearning for it. As the Bible expresses it: 'He has set eternity in the human heart.'[2]

Psalm 90 tries to give us an insight: 'From everlasting to everlasting thou art our God ... A thousand years in thy sight are as yesterday when it is past, and as a watch in the night.'[3] But actually time just leaves us aware of ironies. Our 70 or 80 years are sad and painful and yet we always wish we had more of them: 'The time of our life is threescore years and ten, and if they be of strength, fourscore years: yet their strength is but labour and sorrow: for it is cut off quickly, and we flee away.'[4]

The Bible is positive about time in a way that the sonnet isn't. Despite its impact on each human, time is moving forward with a purpose and God is directing it. Again and again we are asked to view time with a sense of urgency. Isaiah appealed to people that time would one day run out: 'Seek ye the Lord while he may be found: call ye upon him while he is near.'[5] The Day of the Lord was imminent. It was the day when God would bring the events of the time he had created to a climax. His people needed to be ready.

Jesus came, announcing that the moment had come. In the Gospel of Mark he is portrayed as if bursting on to the world's stage, trumpeting God's intervention in human affairs: 'The time is fulfilled, and the kingdom of God is at hand: repent and believe the Gospel.'[6] Paul takes up the theme that there is no time to waste: 'Now is the accepted time, behold now is the day of salvation.'[7]

---

2 Ecclesiastes 3.11 (NIV). The Geneva Bible translates it 'hath set the world in their heart'.

3 Psalm 90.2, 4.

4 Psalm 90.10.

5 Isaiah 55.6.

6 Mark 1.15.

7 2 Corinthians 6.2.

What is the best way to respond to the waves of time making towards the pebbled shore? We return to Psalm 90 for a practical answer. The composer of the psalm makes this request to God: 'Teach us so to number our days, that we may apply our hearts unto wisdom.'[8] Reflecting on our own death is not fashionable. We tend to avoid doing so until circumstances force it upon us. But being aware of the fact that we have only a finite number of days encourages us to use them wisely and to fill each one with a desire for God's eternity.

There will be no Sonnet 60 in heaven. That is, perhaps, a sadness. There will also be no *Taming of the Shrew*. That is, perhaps, a relief. They are creations within time. In the direct presence of God, which is the destiny of us all, they will not be needed. Poetry allows us to apprehend things that we cannot comprehend; things we can only glimpse out of focus in the corner of an eye. No matter what clarity, what beauty, what joy poetry brings, it will be exceeded inestimably by the beauty that awaits us in God. He will make all things plain once and for all. That is the purpose of time rolling forward. That is what we are asked to prepare for with such urgency. In human time, all great art, including drama and poetry, is a gift that helps us prepare. Treasure every minute; treasure every line.

Time has been kind to William. Ben Jonson wrote a poem as part of the prologue to the *First Folio*. He called it 'To the Memory of My Beloved the Author, Mr. William Shakespeare'. Its most memorable line is: 'He was not of an age, but for all time.' The prediction of Sonnet 60 has been fulfilled.

---

8 Psalm 90.12.

Day 23

Out, damned spot! Out, I say!

DOCTOR: Look, how she rubs her hands.

GENTLEWOMAN: It is an accustomed action with her, to seem thus washing her hands: I have known her continue in this a quarter of an hour.

LADY MACBETH: Yet here's a spot.

DOCTOR: Hark! she speaks: I will set down what comes from her, to satisfy my remembrance the more strongly.

LADY MACBETH: Out, damned spot! out, I say! One: two: why, then, 'tis time to do't. Hell is murky! Fie, my lord, fie! a soldier, and afeard? What need we fear who knows it, when none can call our power to account? Yet who would have thought the old man to have had so much blood in him.

DOCTOR: Do you mark that?

LADY MACBETH: The Thane of Fife had a wife: where is she now? What, will these hands ne'er be clean? No more o' that, my lord, no more o' that: you mar all with this starting.

DOCTOR: Go to, go to; you have known what you should not.

GENTLEWOMAN: She has spoke what she should not, I am sure of that: heaven knows what she has known.

LADY MACBETH: Here's the smell of the blood still: all the perfumes of Arabia will not sweeten this little hand. Oh, oh, oh!

Macbeth, Act 5, Scene 1

The woman who says these words is sleepwalking during a nightmare. She has done terrible things and the guilt of them has overwhelmed her. Most of us don't murder a king. But most of us have done things we regret and it is very difficult to stop the memory of them troubling us. Sometimes very deeply. Oh, oh, oh!

Macbeth is the shortest and paciest of Shakespeare's tragedies. It's the story of a man whose thirst for power brings a kingdom to the verge of destruction. It is, you may not be surprised to learn, my favourite of Shakespeare's plays.

Macbeth and another soldier called Banquo are Scottish war heroes, lauded by their king, Duncan. (All three really existed just before the time of the Norman Conquest but, although it was a murderous era, the story is not historically accurate.) Macbeth and Banquo encounter three witches who tell them that Macbeth will become Thane of Cawdor (a thane is a senior nobleman) and then King of Scotland. Banquo's children will also become kings. Macbeth dismisses it. But then Duncan rewards him for his battle valour by making him Thane of Cawdor. It lodges the thought in Macbeth's mind that if the first part of the witches' prophecy has been fulfilled, the other parts might also be.

He sends a letter to his wife, Lady Macbeth, telling her of his swelling ambitions. She makes ready to welcome her husband and the king to their castle. Her fire exceeds Macbeth's and her thoughts turn murderous. Macbeth hesitates, disturbed by portents and visions, but she taunts him to murder Duncan. That night Macbeth stabs the king while he is asleep and puts the blame on his bodyguards, claiming that he caught and killed them in the act. Duncan's son Malcolm and his loyal nobleman Macduff flee to England.

Macbeth becomes King of Scotland, but he is still disturbed by the second part of the witches' prophecy, which was that Banquo's children would become kings. Steeled by the ease with which a murder has handed him the crown, he hires assassins to murder Banquo. They succeed, but his son escapes. That night the ghost of Banquo appears to Macbeth and dread takes hold of him – the start of his downfall.

He revisits the witches and they make three further prophecies. Macbeth will never be harmed by any man born of a woman; he will be safe until the forest called Birnam Wood begins to move; and he must beware Macduff. Macbeth knows enough about childbirth and forestry to assume that he is safe from the first two, but the fact that Macduff is still at large is a threat to him. He has his family murdered. (This is what Lady Macbeth is referring to when she cries, 'The Thane of Fife had a wife: where is she now?') There is no going back: 'I am in blood / Stepped in so far that, should I wade no more, / Returning were as tedious as go o'er.'[1]

Macduff, however, is alive. He is in England, where he has met with Malcolm. He is distraught at the death of his wife and children and enraged to learn that Macbeth has created tyranny in his homeland. He and Malcolm gather allies for an invasion. Lady Macbeth, meanwhile, has been seized by night-terrors, as today's scene makes plain.

Even if the words were in an unknown language we would know that she is in turmoil. Most of the rest of the play is in stately iambic pentameters. The witches cast their spells in short couplets with a driving rhythm: 'Double, double, toil and trouble, / Fire burn and cauldron bubble.'[2] But Lady Macbeth here is barely even using prose. These are fragments of broken thought. The ideas skip from one fractured memory of an earlier event in the play to another, just as images collide but coalesce in a dream.

The pitiless resolve she had earlier in the play, which was the driving force behind the plot to kill Duncan, has disappeared. When Macbeth returned from killing Duncan, covered with blood, she had dismissed his fear: 'A little water clears us of this deed: / How easy is it, then!'[3] But now she can see blood that isn't even there and nothing she can do will remove it.

Shakespeare has taken the association of bloodstained hands with guilt straight from the Bible. In the Old Testament, Isaiah is ferocious in convicting God's people of their wrongdoing: 'When you shall stretch out your hands, I will hide mine eyes

---

1 Act 3, Scene 4.
2 Act 4, Scene 1.
3 Act 2, Scene 2.

from you: and though ye make many prayers, I will not hear: for your hands are full of blood.'[4] In the Gospels, Pilate washes his hands in front of the mob baying for an execution in a futile effort to show himself innocent of Jesus' death. But blood sticks. And it smells – 'all the perfumes of Arabia' will not stop the stench.

The speech is full of references to images that have appeared previously in the play. When her thoughts were turning deadly towards the beginning of the play, Lady Macbeth summoned up hell to cloak her actions: 'Come, thick night, / And pall thee in the dunnest smoke of hell, / That my keen knife see not the wound it makes.'[5] By the end of the play she has got what she recklessly wished for and she knows that darkness intimately: 'Hell is murky.' The couple have created a hell of their own.

Immediately after his first murder, Macbeth thinks he hears God speak: 'Methought I heard a voice cry "Sleep no more! / Macbeth does murder sleep", the innocent sleep, / Sleep that knits up the ravelled sleeve of care.'[6] In the middle of a tortured night, his wife shows that he heard correctly.

What do we do about the guilt that undermines our sleep and brings back the wrongdoing of years long gone to accuse us over and over again? There is, after all, no need for it. The Bible is adamant that God's forgiveness when we repent of our sin is absolute and eternal. This is how those words of Isaiah about bloodstained hands continue:

Come now, and let us reason together, saith the Lord:
though your sins were as crimson, they shall be made white
as snow:
though they were red like scarlet, they shall be as wool.[7]

There is no suggestion in the Bible that we need to confess the same sin and ask for forgiveness over and over again – the very

---

4 Isaiah 1.15.
5 Act 1, Scene 5.
6 Act 2, Scene 2.
7 Isaiah 1.18.

opposite, in fact. Forgiven sin is deleted from God's hard drive – it is we humans who can't stop ourselves trying to recover data from the recycle bin.

Here are some suggestions. Are you the kind of person who responds to drama? It might help to write down the memory which is gripping you on a piece of paper in an act of confession and then destroy it dramatically – burning it or shredding it.

Are you the kind of person who loves to sing? Then bring to mind the Charles Wesley hymn 'O for a thousand tongues to sing'. Develop as an earworm the line: 'He breaks the power of cancelled sin.' It is a rare line in Christian hymnody because it acknowledges that even cancelled sin can still have a power over us. But Jesus wants to break that power. When you are troubled by memories, use the hymn to sing them out of your system.

Are you the kind of person for whom the Bible is persuasive? Then focus on the reassurance that comes in the book of Psalms: 'As far as the East is from the West: so far hath he removed our sins from us.'[8]

I can't be sure that those suggestions will get rid of the damned spots permanently. But in the middle of the night they may allow you to say, 'no more o' that,' and get back to sleep. Tomorrow we will revisit the play and learn the fate of the Macbeths.

---

8 Psalm 103.12.

Day 24

Tomorrow and tomorrow and tomorrow

SEYTON: The queen, my lord, is dead.
MACBETH: She should have died hereafter;
There would have been a time for such a word.
Tomorrow, and tomorrow, and tomorrow,
Creeps in this petty pace from day to day
To the last syllable of recorded time,
And all our yesterdays have lighted fools
The way to dusty death. Out, out, brief candle!
Life's but a walking shadow, a poor player
That struts and frets his hour upon the stage
And then is heard no more: it is a tale
Told by an idiot, full of sound and fury,
Signifying nothing.

Macbeth, Act 5, Scene 5

'Knock knock! Who's there?'

The first known use of this phrase is in *Macbeth*. It doesn't follow the modern formula of the joke, but it is in a comic scene – a release of tension by a drunken porter after the murder of the king.[1] Very many phrases first recorded in this play are familiar today: 'no such thing', 'a sorry sight', 'one fell swoop', 'poisoned chalice', 'the be all and end all'. Four centuries later they have become household words (which is also a phrase coined by Shakespeare). Listing them all would be too much of a good thing (which is also a phrase coined by Shakespeare as luck would have it … which is also a phrase coined by Shakespeare), but what's done is done (which is also a phrase coined

---

1 Act 2, Scene 3.

by Shakespeare). There are approaching 2,000 of his invented words and phrases in everyday use so I shall stop now or we will be here forever and a day. (Ahem!)

Yesterday we read the final words of Lady Macbeth, terrorized in the night by the guilt of what she has done. Today we learn how her husband greets the news of her death. We later discover that it was suicide. Macbeth, nearing despair, clings to the prophecy he was given by the witches. His fate is that he will not be defeated until Birnam Wood begins to move and that no man born of a woman will ever kill him. But in theatrical twists, as the play reaches its climax the wood does move and Macbeth encounters someone to whom a woman did not give birth. Destiny is sealed for a warrior whose ambition so clouded his judgement that he came to suppose that 'fair is foul and foul is fair'.[2]

Today's speech follows a shriek heard elsewhere in the castle. At one time, Macbeth confides in the audience, a scream in the night such as that would have chilled him, but he has known so many horrors that abominations don't disturb him anymore. When the news arrives that the woman he loves is dead, he brushes it aside with the thought that death is inevitable. If it hadn't happened today it would have happened another day. Perhaps tomorrow.

The words that follow have become one of Shakespeare's best-known speeches and it demonstrates how Lady Macbeth's death is the event that finally empties him of anything but pessimism. 'Tomorrow and tomorrow and tomorrow' beats like the pounding of a hammer and then the sound of the double-e of 'creeps' forces the actor's voice as flat as a pulverized body. The days drag on until the end of time. And every day gone by ('all our yesterdays') has served merely to take humans, who are just fools, closer to their death. Macbeth's reference to 'dusty death' here is a quote from the same desolate psalm that Jesus quoted in his dying hours: 'Thou hast brought me into the dust of death.'[3]

---

2 Act 1, Scene 1.
3 Psalm 22.15.

The play is actually full of phrases that are reminiscent of the Geneva Bible which Shakespeare knew best. In this speech, for example, two of his images were taken together from the dismaying advice given to Job by one of his so-called friends: 'We are but of yesterday, and are ignorant: for our days upon earth are but a shadow.'[4]

The imagery in the second half of the speech doesn't come from the Bible, though, but from the theatre. Life is 'a poor player / That struts and frets his hour upon the stage'. This is an actor on a stage reminding us that he is an actor on a stage. The performance that seems so real is illusory and when the performers leave it is gone for ever and 'is heard no more'. Equally, a human life, which seems so vivid and important during its span, will disappear leaving nothing behind. It is just the meaningless noise and emotion of an idiot, 'signifying nothing'.

Anarchic though this is, there is something self-justifying about Macbeth's words here. If everything is meaningless then the evil of his crimes is less awful. In the eternal scheme of things they signify nothing, just like everything else.

It is impossible to know whether, at this stage of his career, this sense of abject emptiness is something that Shakespeare knew for himself or if it's the creation of a brilliant imagination. In the timeline of his plays, *Macbeth* comes in the middle of a period in which tragedies are unrelenting. One thing that is certain, though, is that the speech is in absolute contrast to a Christian worldview.

Life is not meaningless. And life is not an accident. There is purpose and meaning to every human existence, whether a child lives a few heartbreaking hours or a grandfather attempts a wobbly dance on his ninetieth birthday.

One thing that Christians share with the context of the play is that there is a supernatural dimension to existence which cannot be ignored. However, it isn't the world of witches and ghosts that Macbeth encountered; it is a world in which there

---

4 Job 8.9.

is a God who has always existed and needed no one to create him. Science is able to tell us what exists and how; we look to God to tell us why it exists and what it means.

We believe that everything that is, that ever has been and ever will be, has been brought into existence because God willed it. Our planet is unique, statistically improbable and very different from the rest of the known universe. It's a planet specifically designed for life. Six hundred years before Jesus, the prophet Isaiah wrote:

> The Lord that created heaven, God himself that formed the earth, and made it: he that prepared it, he created it not in vain: he formed it to be inhabited.[5]

But God is more than an impersonal force creating a universe. God created human beings in order for them to share in his own existence. Human beings and all of creation exist to show God's glory. And that will be true tomorrow and tomorrow and tomorrow.

The Bible describes human beings as singled out for special status. We are made 'in the image of God'.[6] It is not in any sense a physical likeness, but a capacity to engage in life mentally, morally, creatively, socially and spiritually. The image of God distinguishes humans from the remainder of the animal, mineral and vegetable world and enables them to enter into an active relationship with their maker. It is also that image which makes it iniquitous to rob another human being of life, no matter what vaulting ambition presents itself.

The whole Bible tells the story of God's relationship of love with his creation. Jesus spoke of the overwhelming significance of love. When he was asked to say which were the most important of God's commandments, he selected two – to love God and to love other people.[7] Everything that gives life meaning

---

5 Isaiah 45.18.
6 Genesis 1.26.
7 Matthew 22.36–40.

follows from those. The reason for and the fulfilment of our existence is love.

Despite every nihilistic word that Macbeth speaks as fate seems to lead him inexorably from one depravity to the next, I believe that in my heart of hearts (which is also a phrase coined by Shakespeare).

Day 25

This blessed plot, this earth, this realm, this England

JOHN OF GAUNT:
This royal throne of kings, this sceptered isle,
This earth of majesty, this seat of Mars,
This other Eden, demi-paradise,
This fortress built by Nature for herself
Against infection and the hand of war,
This happy breed of men, this little world,
This precious stone set in the silver sea,
Which serves it in the office of a wall,
Or as a moat defensive to a house,
Against the envy of less happier lands,
This blessed plot, this earth, this realm, this England,
This nurse, this teeming womb of royal kings,
Feared by their breed and famous by their birth,
Renowned for their deeds as far from home,
For Christian service and true chivalry,
As is the sepulchre in stubborn Jewry,
Of the world's ransom, blessed Mary's Son,
This land of such dear souls, this dear dear land.

Richard II, Act 2, Scene 1

And at that point the speech could go one of two ways. It is a paean to England as a great nation. It is spoken by a man who is gravely ill and desperate to say something that is important to him. Its mellifluent images make it so memorable that within five years it was being published in anthologies, even though the play had fallen out of favour. John of Gaunt could either go on to say that 1399 is England's finest hour, or that everything good that he mentions is wrecked.

According to him, England's greatness lies in its historic succession of kings (it is a 'sceptered' island). The wars it has survived have made it what it is (the 'seat of Mars', the Roman god of war). It is so like a paradise that it rivals God's perfect Eden. It is a 'precious stone' which, because it's an island, has kept plagues and invasions at bay. Other countries on the mainland of Europe do not have these advantages, which makes them 'less happier lands'. The rhetoric reaches its height with four ideas crammed into a single line: 'This blessed plot, this earth, this realm, this England.' He's a dying man. He can't waste a syllable. The repeated 'this' thwacks like a drumbeat in a victory parade.

England's kings, he says, are acclaimed far and wide. This is because they use their position for 'Christian service'. Their gallantry is so well known that the only thing equally famous is the tomb of Jesus in Jerusalem. (Jewry is 'stubborn' in this speech because the Jews have not recognized Jesus to be their Saviour.)

So which of the two ways does the speech go? John of Gaunt is caustic. What was once a great nation has been rented out like a studio flat or a factory farm ('I die pronouncing it like to a tenement or a pelting farm'). King Richard II is wholly to blame. He is wasteful, in love with the trappings of monarchy, out of touch with his subjects and infatuated with a trio of young, handsome men. And he has grievously wounded John by banishing his son Bolingbroke. 'England, that was wont to conquer others, / Hath made a shameful conquest of itself.'

Richard II is the last king of England in the Plantagenet line. After the death of John of Gaunt, he seizes his land and money in order to finance a war in Ireland. Both noblemen and commoners of England realize that this time he has gone too far, but most of all it enrages John's exiled son Bolingbroke, who is held in high esteem. With Richard away in Ireland, he assembles an army and invades Yorkshire. One by one, Richard's allies defect and join him. By the time Richard returns he has lost his grip on the country. Bolingbroke has him arrested and brought to London. He is crowned king in his place. The name he takes upon assuming the throne is Henry IV, the king whose troubled relationship with his son Harry was the subject of the two plays we looked at a week ago.

Who has right on his side? Is it Richard, who is selfish, autocratic and up himself, but nevertheless the legitimate king? Or is it Bolingbroke, who is charismatic, talented and popular, but a usurper? Richard publicly hands his crown and sceptre to Bolingbroke. He compares the betrayal he is experiencing to the suffering of Jesus, only worse: 'Did they not sometime cry 'All hail!' to me? / So Judas did to Christ. But He in twelve / Found truth in all but one; I in twelve thousand, none.'[1] However, everything he says is so poetically luxurious with self-pity that our sympathies waver.

Refusing to confess that he has committed crimes against his country, Richard is imprisoned in Pomfret Castle. One of the ambitious noblemen in the court of the new Henry IV hears him speak of Richard as a 'living fear'. He travels to Pomfret and murders the former king – an act that secures Henry's position but torments him for the rest of his life.

Richard II was written and performed during the last decade of the life of Elizabeth I at a time when, without a husband or an heir, the question of who would succeed her was acute. The play became entangled in a notable political disturbance. The Earl of Essex, who was once Elizabeth's favourite, had been placed under house arrest because he had exceeded his authority as Lieutenant of Ireland. He planned a coup.

On 7 February 1601, he commissioned a performance of *Richard II* at the Globe, with express instructions that it should include the scenes in which the monarch was deposed and killed. The next day, Essex, with 300 men behind him, set off from his home (near where Charing Cross Station now stands) towards the Tower of London, planning to take it and use the authority it gave him to arrest the queen. He was confident that thousands of people would rally behind him as he rode. In fact,

---

1 Act 4, Scene 1.

no one did. The streets emptied. A handful of startled soldiers took pot-shots at him. After stopping for lunch he realized that his army was peeling away, so he went back home and started destroying incriminating documents. He was arrested and beheaded.

During the investigation that followed, Shakespeare's company, the Chamberlain's Men, were called to give evidence. They persuaded the court that they had been innocently duped into performing the provocative play. They were obviously believed, because the queen commanded a performance from them at her palace the night before the execution.

Richard II ends with Henry IV vowing to seek God's forgiveness for his part in the death of the rightful king. To do so he will 'make a voyage to the Holy Land'[2] and lead a crusade to retake Jerusalem from Muslim rule. He never did so. In fact, the last crusade in which combatants from England had a significant part was the inconclusive 9th Crusade, 130 years previously.

Today, the Christian church in the England that John of Gaunt loved is not characterized by violence against its opponents. The same is true for most of the Christian world, which makes it shocking when news of violent actions by churchgoing people is broadcast. Unlike the centuries of Richard II or Shakespeare, murderous Christians are extremely rare. For this I thank God.

What went right? Enlightenment happened. This eighteenth-century philosophical movement changed the way we examine our concepts of truth, right and wrong. Progress was driven by raw, logical thought. It was fired not by supernatural beliefs, but by science, analysis and the pursuit of good for every member of society. Whether or not we realize it, our worldview has been forged by bringing this rational, humanist thinking to the Christian faith. It civilized the Church. It made us what we are.

The UK of the nineteenth century had a revolution. Unlike other European 'less happier' revolutions, it did not involve violence. Rather, we built sewers, reformed prisons, created

---

2 Act 5, Scene 6.

a network of railways, made child labour illegal, founded art galleries and eradicated smallpox. Each of those social reforms was driven by Christian men and women who were doing it because the way of Jesus had taken hold of their lives. They didn't make much of it. They were wishy-washy Christians. But they brought healing, compassion, justice and the casting out of demons – the signs by which Jesus said that people would recognize the Kingdom of God.

I am a fervent believer in wishy-washy Christianity. Strident Christianity brought us the Crusades; wishy-washy Christianity brought us the Welfare State, the end of legalized slavery and a justice system in which politically inconvenient people are not murdered in Pomfret Castle.

Being a wishy-washy Christian is hard work. It means committing yourself to things in the life of the neighbourhood you would rather not do. It means you vote (even though you really would rather not engage with the leaflets that tumble through your letterbox). It means you visit the lonely (even though your time is the commodity you can least spare). It means you join Parent Teacher Associations, unions and the Neighbourhood Watch (even though they involve the most boring meetings known to humankind). It means you extend hospitality to people you wouldn't usually invite into your home (even though you would prefer not to have your sofa smell of wee). And it means you befriend your neighbours (even if they are not churchgoers).

I am John of Gaunt. I absolutely love England. Don't misunderstand me – I also have a very great love of Scotland, Wales and Northern Ireland. There are many places in the world that I have a great affection for, but I am a patriot. It is unfashionable to say this.

It is even more unfashionable to say that I love the churches of the land in which I was born – those broad, tolerant, agonizing, welcoming, civilized, prayerful churches that have been central to making this a good country in which to live. I don't want to go anywhere else. I want to be here, and I want the deep love I feel for Jesus to inspire me to make this place a 'dear dear land'.

Day 26

As flies to wanton boys are we to the gods

GLOUCESTER: Is it a beggarman?
OLD MAN: Madman and beggar too.
GLOUCESTER: He has some reason, else he could not beg.
In the last night's storm I such a fellow saw,
Which made me think a man a worm. My son
Came then into my mind, and yet my mind
Was then scarce friends with him. I have heard more since.
As flies to wanton boys are we to the gods.
They kill us for their sport.

King Lear, Act 4, Scene 1

Early in the play that bears his name, King Lear asks: 'Who is it that can tell me who I am?'[1] It's a request for flattery from a man who wants to be told that he is loved. But the question echoes through the play as an exploration of what it means to be human. And the answer is as bleak about the human condition as anything ever written.

King Lear was a king of Britain (in legend and perhaps in reality) many centuries before Jesus, at about the time Amos was cursing injustice against the poor. The play is about how a headstrong old man, blind to his weaknesses, is stripped of everything that gives worth to his life and finds a scrap of understanding, but too late to save himself or anyone in his circle from a wretched death.

Lear has three daughters and plans to abdicate, dividing his kingdom into three based on how eloquently they praise him. Goneril and Regan, lips smacking with greed, fabricate

---

1 Act 1, Scene 4.

their affection. Cordelia, the youngest and his favourite, recognizes their hypocrisy and refuses to join in the charade. Lear is infuriated and banishes her, thus casting out someone whose love for him is deep and genuine.

He makes himself a guest at Goneril's castle, but she is a vile and unwilling host. Her servants are so insulting to him that he leaves in a fury. At Regan's castle he is treated with equal disdain and, unable to comprehend why his daughters are betraying him, he begins to lose his senses. Homeless, he heads out on to the heath where, in a storm, he descends into insanity. His Fool, who dares to speak the truth to him, and Kent, a nobleman who stays loyal to the end, accompany him.

In a parallel subplot, the Earl of Gloucester has two sons. In an attempt to steal an inheritance, the illegitimate son Edmund persuades him that the son he loves dearly, Edgar, is attempting to kill him. Gloucester sends men after Edgar so he disguises himself as a mad beggar, naked but for a blanket, and flees. He too makes for the heath. There in the gale he and Lear meet – two people brought as low as humanity can go. 'Unaccommodated man is no more but such a poor, bare, forked animal as thou art.'[2]

Realizing what has happened to Lear, Gloucester goes to Regan to try to help him. She accuses him of treason and, in a truly horrific scene, rips out his eyes. Thrown out to wander the countryside, he is discovered by his son Edgar, who does not reveal his true identity. Gloucester tries to commit suicide, but Edgar saves him. They are reunited and, overcome with both joy and sorrow, Gloucester dies.

In Dover, Cordelia leads a French army to take England from the hands of her sisters. They are defeated and both she and Lear are taken captive. He realizes the truth of what has happened and they cling to each other with love restored.

Edmund, meanwhile, is having affairs with both Regan and Goneril. Goneril poisons her sister out of jealousy and then kills herself. Edgar throws off his disguise, fights a duel with Edmund and kills him. As Edmund dies, he reveals that he has

---

2 Act 3, Scene 4.

ordered Cordelia's execution. There is a rush to save her, but it's too late. Lear carries the body of his daughter on to the stage. She will never breathe again. As if there is no longer any point in forming sentences, Lear groans: 'Never, never, never, never, never.'[3] (The metre is the reverse of the iambs in which most of Shakespeare's verse is written. The stress pounds repeatedly on the first syllable of the word. The technical term for this is five trochees. The non-technical term is five wallops to your emotions.) The king dies grief-stricken.

Yes, that's bleak. So bleak, in fact, that for nearly two centuries that ending wasn't performed. In 1681, Nahum Tate, who was the Poet Laureate, rewrote *King Lear* and changed the conclusion. In his version, Lear and Gloucester, chastened and enlightened by their experiences, survive. Their children, Cordelia and Edgar, marry and lead England into recovery. This adaptation was the version performed until 1838. There were understandable reasons for Tate's version. Just over 30 years after Shakespeare died, King Charles I was executed following a civil war and theatre was outlawed. When the monarchy was restored, King Charles II encouraged theatres to reopen. Both the politics and the mood of the time were suited to a story in which King Lear is restored to his throne.

Nahum Tate took a play that is almost unbearable and made it hopeful but flat-footed. It was not until the twentieth century, when it became clear that human beings have a previously unimaginable capacity for cruelty and slaughter, that Shakespeare's original version began once more to speak insightfully into the understanding and conscience of audiences. The horror, and our response to it, became a compelling reason to engage with the play.

Today's speech comes when Gloucester has been blinded. In blindness he comes to see the emptiness of power and the need for compassion. With a similar irony, Lear, in his madness, comes to his senses about his true nature and what it means to give and accept love. The 'beggarman' who Gloucester encounters is his son Edgar. He had seen him in 'last night's storm' in

---

3 Act 5, Scene 3.

such a desolate state that it seemed that being human brought with it no more dignity than being an earthworm. The image is a reference to Psalm 22, the words of which Jesus cried as he was being killed. The psalm is the groan of a man in such physical and spiritual pain that it seems God has forsaken him: 'I am a worm, and not a man: a shame of men, and the contempt of the people. All they that see me have me in derision.'[4]

Poignantly, Gloucester reveals that when he saw the beggar the previous evening he thought he glimpsed Edgar's likeness, but in his anger he did not mention it because he was 'scarce friends' with someone he thought was plotting against him. He knows better now ('I have heard more since'). And then comes his devastating pronouncement: 'As flies to wanton boys are we to the gods. / They kill us for their sport.' This is not a world in which there is no god. It's worse. There are indeed gods, but they are completely loveless. Their only interest in humans is a perverted desire to watch how they react when they are made to suffer.

The play is set in pre-Christian times, which gives Shakespeare the opportunity to explore the idea that there is no justice in the universe without being accused of blasphemy. When Edgar draws his sword to duel Edmund in the play's closing scene he declares, 'The gods are just.'[5] But everything we have seen tells us that he is deceiving himself. The good die alongside the wicked and Gloucester's cynicism is the only meaning we are offered to account for the intolerable suffering that pervades the play. *King Lear* is the biblical story of Job, but with no hint of restoration at the end of his torment. It is Good Friday with no Easter.

'Who is it that can tell me who I am?' The pagan gods of Lear's world gave him a desolate account of who he is. The Christian God gives an altogether different assessment of human flesh and bone. The one who can truly tell you who you are is your Creator:

---

4 Psalm 22.6, 7.
5 Act 5, Scene 3.

I will praise thee, for I am fearfully and wondrously made:
marvellous are thy works, and my soul knoweth it well.
My bones are not hid from thee, though I was made in a
  secret place.[6]

These words come from Psalm 139 and they speak of a Creator
who is intimately invested in the life of every individual. Even
within the womb, that secret place, God knew you, understood
you and began to guide you. The psalm acknowledges that life
will lead you into hellish places. However, in those tortured
times you will not be alone:

Thither shall thine hand lead me, and thy right hand hold me.
If I say, Yet the darkness shall hide me, even the night shall
  be light about me.[7]

Four centuries of science since *King Lear* was written have led
many to a different conclusion from that of Gloucester. Many
make their way through their days without a meaningful ref-
erence to a god of any kind. A godless view of the body sees it
merely as a vehicle for reproducing more life through as much
sex as possible. However, a Christian view of the body sees it
as something to cherish.

Jesus dignified the human body fearfully and wondrously
by choosing to inhabit one when he walked and talked on our
planet. That has implications for the most basic activities of
our lives. It means that sex is more than just an animal urge,
but something to be enjoyed imaginatively and passionately in
a relationship of love. It means that human bodies have pur-
pose and value. Blind bodies like Gloucester's are precious.
Mentally ill bodies like Lear's are precious. Vulnerable bodies
like Edgar's are precious. Abused bodies like Cordelia's are
precious.

---

6 Psalm 139.14, 15.
7 Psalm 139.11, 12.

Four centuries of science, however, have told us nothing about the ways of the human heart that Shakespeare did not already know. Before the lives around them are snuffed out, Lear and Cordelia are allowed a moment in which they discover that their world is not meaningless, because love matters. As they depart for a prison cell, Lear tells his daughter: 'When thou dost ask me blessing, I'll kneel down / And ask of thee forgiveness. So we'll live, / And pray, and sing.'[8] It's not much in the context of such anguish, but as a Christian, I'll take it.

<hr/>

8 Act 5, Scene 3.

Day 27

What a piece of work is a man!

HAMLET: I have of late – but wherefore I know not – lost
all my mirth, forgone all custom of exercises; and indeed, it
goes so heavily with my disposition that this goodly frame,
the earth, seems to me a sterile promontory; this most
excellent canopy, the air, look you, this brave o'erhanging
firmament, this majestical roof fretted with golden fire –
why, it appeareth no other thing to me than a foul and
pestilent congregation of vapours. What a piece of work
is a man! How noble in reason! How infinite in faculties!
In form and moving how express and admirable! In action
how like an angel! In apprehension how like a god! The
beauty of the world, the paragon of animals! And yet to me
what is this quintessence of dust?

Hamlet, Act 2, Scene 2

We are back where we began. Dust!

Who is this man, so depressed that the finest things that life
can offer seem like they have been crushed into dust? He is
Hamlet. He is the Prince of Denmark.

He says he doesn't know why he is so melancholy and has
stopped doing any sport ('all custom of exercises'). But that's
not the truth. He does know why. He has come home from
university because his father has died. And he is increasingly
convinced that he was murdered.

Hamlet looks at the awe-inspiring sky on a day glorious
with sunshine ('this majestical roof fretted with golden fire'). It
might as well be smog (a 'congregation of vapours'). He looks
at human beings – noble, admirable, beautiful. What they

are capable of doing is little short of what angels do. Their intelligence ('apprehension') is practically godlike. But despite knowing this, he feels like dirt.

This wonderfully graceful and thought-provoking speech is in prose. This is unusual for Shakespeare, who mostly uses prose for comedy, chit-chat or madness. Perhaps, ever the innovator, he wants to show how rich and resonant prose can be. Or perhaps Hamlet actually is mad – he has told his best friend that in order to find out how his father died he is going to pretend that his wits are unravelling ('an antic disposition').[1]

What books has Hamlet been reading? The ideas about humans being God's greatest creation were influenced by an Italian philosopher called Giovanni Pico della Mirandola, who wrote a book called *Oration on the Dignity of Man* a century previously. The scepticism about human worth came from a French intellectual called Michel de Montaigne, who had recently died. But the text that Shakespeare clearly had in his head on the day he composed this speech is Psalm 8 – an outpouring of joy at the majesty of God.

> When I behold thine heavens, even the works of thy fingers,
> The moon and the stars, which thou hast ordained,
> What is man, say I, that thou art mindful of him?
> And the son of man that thou visitest him?
> For thou hast made him a little lower than God,
> And crowned him with glory and worship.[2]

When the psalm was written, astronomy was a brand-new science. In Babylon, scientists were beginning to map the night sky and already had tables accurately predicting lunar eclipses. When *Hamlet* was written, Shakespeare was encountering the thinking of the astronomer Thomas Digges, who furthered the discovery that the earth revolves around the sun by suggesting that stars are not resting on a crystal sphere, as had previously

---

1 Act 1, Scene 5.
2 Psalm 8.3–5.

been thought, but extend into 'infinite space' (a phrase that Hamlet uses earlier in the scene to describe the extent of his imagination).

To the believer, then as now, this results in awe at the magnificence of God and his love for humanity. To the sceptic, it affirms the impossibility of a creator being responsible for such an insignificant thing as human life on planet Earth. Although they answer it in different ways, at heart they are both asking the same question. What on earth have humans done to deserve all this? Or rather, 'What a piece of work is a man!'

The reason Hamlet thinks his father was murdered is that he has seen his ghost. The ghost tells him that the present king, his uncle Claudius, slithered like a serpent through Eden into the garden where he was asleep and poisoned him. He then married his widow, Hamlet's mother Gertrude. The ghost implores Hamlet to avenge his death.

This would have set up an expectation in Shakespeare's first audience that the play would follow the pattern of revenge tragedies, which were popular in the sixteenth century. They featured a hero who loses his life in the pursuit of revenge for the death of someone he loves. Familiar themes in these plays were madness, grotesque deaths and supernatural appearances. Most sixteenth-century playwrights embellished the revenge tragedy genre with gore and titillation. In *Hamlet*, Shakespeare embellished it with exploration of the fear of death, the torment of doubt and the chasm between intentions and action. It is a class apart.

The change in Hamlet's temperament worries Claudius and Gertrude, so they pay two of his university friends to keep watch on him – Rosencrantz and Guildenstern. Their pompous Lord Chamberlain, Polonius, thinks he is acting as he is because something has gone wrong in his relationship with his girlfriend, Polonius' daughter Ophelia. Certainly Hamlet is not treating her with the love they once shared; he is almost cruel.

When a troupe of travelling actors arrives at the castle, Hamlet hits upon an idea to find out for certain whether Claudius did indeed kill his father. He asks them to perform a play that includes a scene in which someone is murdered in circumstances very similar to those in which he believes his father died. As he suspected, when that moment comes Claudius leaps up and leaves the room in a state of agitation. It is proof and it steels Hamlet to kill him.

He hunts for the king throughout the palace and finds him saying his prayers. He creeps up behind him, weapon in hand. But a thought makes him hesitate. If he kills Claudius while he is praying his soul will go to heaven. What kind of revenge is that? The moment to kill him with certainty that Claudius will go to hell is while he is drunk or blaspheming or having sex with Hamlet's mother. What should he do? Tomorrow we will revisit the play and find out the consequences of Hamlet's indecision.

Today, however, we must come to terms with an irony. Claudius tells us that he was not praying after all. He has been trying to mouth the words, but he knows that God cannot possibly forgive him because the truth is that he does not repent. He knows that 'my offence is rank, it smells to heaven',[3] but he will never be persuaded to part with the things for which he committed the crime – the stolen crown, the stolen wife and the pitiless ambition.

Here he is, acknowledging that for all a human may have action like an angel and apprehension like a god, these things do not impress God. The only acceptable way to come to God is to stop relying on a steely heart and instead approach him with the helplessness of a baby: 'O wretched state! O bosom black as death! ... / Bow, stubborn knees; and heart with strings of steel, / Be soft as sinews of the new-born babe!'[4]

And that brings us back to Psalm 8:

O Lord our Lord, how excellent is thy Name in all the world!
Which hast set thy glory above the heavens.

---

3 Act 3, Scene 3.
4 Act 3, Scene 3.

Out of the mouth of babes and sucklings hast thou ordained
strength, because of thine enemies,
That thou mightest still the enemy and the avenger.[5]

Regardless of whether 'this brave o'erhanging firmament'
strengthens a belief in God or does the opposite, there is some-
one whose thoughts are even more powerful than a psalmist or
an astronomer or a prince of Denmark. That is a baby. He or
she doesn't attempt to explain God, or measure him, or reject
him. A baby just wonders.

Nobody – not even God's worst enemy – would say to an
infant that it's ridiculous to be in awe of what is just a random
evolutionary blip in the great godless progress of the cosmos.
Instead a child is encouraged to marvel.

Baby one; sceptic nil.

The difference between Hamlet's version of Psalm 8 and the
original is the absence of worship. Without an acknowledge-
ment of the greatness of the Creator, the blazing splendour
of the heavens and the loveliness of human achievement are
just air and dust. A touch of childish astonishment would be
an enlivening way to draw near to God at this stage of our
journey through Lent.

---

5 Psalm 8.1, 2.

Day 28

To be or not to be – that is the question

HAMLET: To be, or not to be – that is the question:
Whether 'tis nobler in the mind to suffer
The slings and arrows of outrageous fortune
Or to take arms against a sea of troubles,
And by opposing end them. To die – to sleep –
No more; and by a sleep to say we end
The heartache, and the thousand natural shocks
That flesh is heir to. 'Tis a consummation
Devoutly to be wished. To die – to sleep.
To sleep – perchance to dream: ay, there's the rub!
For in that sleep of death what dreams may come
When we have shuffled off this mortal coil,
Must give us pause. There's the respect
That makes calamity of so long life.
For who would bear the whips and scorns of time,
Th' oppressor's wrong, the proud man's contumely,
The pangs of despised love, the law's delay,
The insolence of office, and the spurns
That patient merit of th' unworthy takes,
When he himself might his quietus make
With a bare bodkin? Who would these fardels bear,
To grunt and sweat under a weary life,
But that the dread of something after death –
The undiscovered country, from whose bourn
No traveller returns – puzzles the will,
And makes us rather bear those ills we have
Than fly to others that we know not of?

Hamlet, Act 3, Scene 1

William's father died in 1601. John was 70, which was a ripe old age, but he had been a financial failure for nearly 30 years because of bad business choices. His wife Mary outlived him by seven years, but his son Edmund died in his mid-twenties having followed his brother to London to try his hand as an actor. William paid for his funeral in Southwark Cathedral and, ironically, it is the writer who now has an ornate memorial there, close to where Edmund is buried.

While his family's fortunes stuttered, William's soared. He procured more and more property in Stratford and drew attention to his status by securing a coat of arms. He did this at great expense in the name of his father so that he and all his male heirs would be addressed as gentlemen – something that several of his fellow actors sought in order to give them some respectability in a profession routinely associated with ribaldry.

So it was in the context of grief over his father's death that Shakespeare was writing a play about a young prince dealing with the death of his father. Hamlet fails to take revenge on Claudius, the murderer, when the ideal opportunity is presented to him. Instead he confronts his mother Gertrude in her bedroom, in order to tell her what he knows. Hearing a noise behind a tapestry he suspects that Claudius is hiding there and stabs through the material. But it isn't Claudius. It's Polonius, the wearisome courtier who is father to his former girlfriend Ophelia.

Fearing for his safety after Polonius' death, Claudius has Hamlet banished to England. But he sends the prince's friends Rosencrantz and Guildenstern with him bearing orders that he should be executed. Ophelia descends into madness as she grieves for her father and drowns herself in a river.

Hamlet escapes death when the ship bearing him to England is attacked and he makes his way incognito back to Denmark. He first learns of Ophelia's death when he stumbles across her funeral. Her brother Laertes is incensed with rage and holds Hamlet responsible for both her death and his father's. They tumble into Ophelia's grave fighting, until they are pulled apart.

Claudius hatches a plot with Laertes. Like Hamlet, Laertes has the death of a father to avenge. But unlike Hamlet, he has no doubt about what needs to be done. Knowing that Hamlet used to be a lover of sport, Claudius plans an innocent-seeming fencing match. However, the tip of Laertes' sword will be poisoned. If Laertes wins, Hamlet will die from whatever scratch he sustains during the contest. If Hamlet wins, he will be rewarded with a cup of wine which will also be poisoned.

The fencing bout becomes chaotic. The poisoned sword falls into the wrong hands. The wine is drunk by the wrong person. There are many deaths, the last of which is Hamlet himself. He dies in the arms of his best friend, who takes leave of him with the words: 'Now cracks a noble heart. Goodnight, sweet prince, / And flights of angels sing thee to thy rest.'[1]

Rest in peace, Hamlet. This is the most appropriate blessing to offer to a character who was so scared of dying and yet so agonized by living. When both options are unbearable, how can a person possibly decide whether it is better 'to be or not to be'? Is it more noble to put up with the dreadful events that luck throws your way ('the slings and arrows of outrageous fortune') or to win a victory over them by choosing death ('by opposing, end them')?

To die is just to sleep. It's 'no more' than that. It's the end we all want ('a consummation devoutly to be wished'). But there's a catch (a 'rub'). Sleep may seem wonderful, but it's the place where nightmares happen.

In the speech you can hear the precise moment at which the catch occurs to Hamlet. He repeats 'to die, to sleep' as if he is drifting into a reverie. But then he is snapped out of it by a disturbing new thought: 'To sleep, perchance to dream.' An actor saying this most famous of speeches cannot help but convey it precisely as Shakespeare intended if he trusts the rhythm and the repetition. The technical word for ending one line and beginning the next with the same phrase, but emphasized in a different way, is anadiplosis.

---

1 Act 5, Scene 2.

It's not knowing what might happen after we have died ('shuffled off this mortal coil') that makes us put up with our suffering for so long. Hamlet then gives a long list of the 'whips and scorns' that make life so hard to bear – abuse, unrequited love, injustice. Why not just end them by turning your dagger on yourself ('a bare bodkin')? The only thing that keeps us alive is the thought which 'puzzles the will', that death might be worse and the knowledge that whatever it is, it is final. It is 'the undiscovered country, from whose bourn no traveller returns'.

What has made this speech so well known and so quotable? It's the fact that the first six words are so very short and repetitive. It gives the sense that it is the most fundamental and important question a human could ever ask, which perhaps it is. We are being asked to consider our death. We are rarely encouraged to do that. We pay funeral directors and solicitors to do it so that we don't have to. Occasional fears come to us all. Even those of us with a Christian faith cannot pretend to know for sure that there is a joyous life after death, because such things are unknowable.

Hamlet had some beliefs that I emphatically do not share. I don't believe in ghosts. I don't believe I am fated to die in a particular way on a particular day by a god who has decreed that 'there's a special providence in the fall of a sparrow'.[2] I don't believe there is anything at all to be scared of about the mystery of what lies beyond life.

However, I share Hamlet's belief in the Christian God. And I do believe he has good intentions for us, no matter how comprehensively we screw up. Or as he puts it: 'There's a divinity doth shape our ends / Rough-hew them how we will.'[3]

I have come to a quietly assured conclusion that I am going to meet God after I die and will once again meet people whom I have loved. Why? Three reasons.

The first is that Jesus believed in eternal life and I trust him. In fact, he teased those Jews who did not share that belief. He

2 Act 5, Scene 2.
3 Act 5, Scene 2.

faced his own death reluctantly and with ferocious doubts, but resolved that he could submit to what was ahead with trust in the God who brings new life. I find myself persuaded to share his trust.

The second is that something phenomenal happened on the third day after Jesus died. I can't be sure what it was because even the eye witnesses were not sure. They described the Jesus whom they encountered after his death as both a real presence and as a vision that came and went; both a human figure and something utterly different. He was worshipped by some, while others literally couldn't believe their eyes. But whatever it was, something beautiful had reached back to them from beyond the grave and transformed the lives of those left behind in a way that was entirely good and empowering. It was a resurrection.

The third reason is that almost immediately after Jesus ascended, his followers were facing death, comforted and without fear, in the knowledge that they were going to a place where they would meet him again. Christian gravestones that have survived from about the year 80 show the image of a shepherd carrying a sheep and the names of believers who, so soon after Jesus had walked the earth, were going to their deaths with a gentle confidence that they were being carried home.

If death had the last word, we could never be completely fulfilled. But death doesn't have the last word. God is planning to have the last word himself. I don't believe that lightly or without wavering, but I do feel able to let go of life without fear of that 'undiscovered country'.

Hamlet is a truly great play about the most important things in life. The hero is so compelling and believable that I feel as if I have been writing this chapter as a letter to him. Don't be afraid. Your last words were, 'The rest is silence.'[4] You were wrong.

---

4 Act 5, Scene 2.

Day 29

Age cannot wither her, nor custom stale her infinite variety

ENOBARBUS: The barge she sat in, like a burnished throne,
Burned on the water: the poop was beaten gold;
Purple the sails, and so perfumed that
The winds were love-sick with them; the oars were silver,
Which to the tune of flutes kept stroke, and made
The water which they beat to follow faster,
As amorous of their strokes. For her own person,
It beggared all description: she did lie
In her pavilion – cloth-of-gold of tissue –
O'er-picturing that Venus where we see
The fancy outwork nature ... I saw her once
Hop forty paces through the public street;
And having lost her breath, she spoke, and panted,
That she did make defect perfection,
And, breathless, power breathe forth.
MECAENUS: Now Antony must leave her utterly.
ENOBARBUS: Never; he will not:
Age cannot wither her, nor custom stale
Her infinite variety: other women cloy
The appetites they feed: but she makes hungry
Where most she satisfies; for vilest things
Become themselves in her: that the holy priests
Bless her when she is riggish.

Antony and Cleopatra, Act 2, Scene 2

The man who speaks these words is Domitius Enobarbus, who was a politician in Rome about 40 years before the birth of

Jesus. Rome was ruled jointly by three men – Antony, Lepidus and Octavius. Octavius was later renamed Augustus Caesar and it was he who ordered the census which brought Mary and Joseph to Bethlehem.

Enobarbus was ferociously loyal to Antony. The woman he describes here in awed tones was the Queen of Egypt, 1,200 miles from Rome. Her passionate love affair with Antony was both their glory and their downfall. Her name was Cleopatra.

Enobarbus is depicting the first time Antony clapped eyes on Cleopatra, as she sailed up the River Cydnus on a golden barge. Flutes are playing. The sails are drenched in perfume. Cleopatra, managing her public image as scrupulously as any Hollywood star, presents herself as a goddess. Enobarbus is awe-struck. You know how an artist paints the goddess Venus with such beauty that it would be impossible in real life ('we see the fancy outwork nature')? Well, Cleopatra was even more beautiful ('o'er-picturing that').

Is she perfect? Well, once she hopped down a street so fast that she was breathless. (What a performer!) She made it seem like being out of breath wasn't an imperfection, but was the most powerful way a human could be.

Antony is never going to leave her, declares Enobarbus. (This is a prediction that comes true again and again throughout the play and finally undoes them both.) The passing of the years won't make her any less stunning ('age cannot wither her'). And no matter how long he is with her, she will never grow boring ('infinite variety'). The more you see her the more you want her ('she makes hungry where most she satisfies'). She is so wondrous that even the worst of her is charming.

Saints preserve us! Actually, they'll have to because the priests are so in her thrall that when she behaves like a jezebel ('riggish') they give her their blessing.

At the start of the play, Antony and Cleopatra are already miles deep in love. It's only the death of his wife and the news of an army being raised to overthrow the three leaders that snaps Antony away from his decadent life in Egypt and takes him home to Rome. The triumvirate realize that they need a sign of unity to strengthen their grip on power, so Antony marries Octavius' sister, Octavia. Enobarbus predicts that it won't stop him returning to Cleopatra. He's right, of course.

Internal arguments and external wars divide the three and threaten the grip they have on power. Octavia pleads with Antony to be reconciled with her brother so that she doesn't have impossibly divided loyalties. Antony sends her to Octavius in Rome on a peace mission. When she is out of the way, guess where he goes!

In Egypt, he is reunited with Cleopatra and together they mobilize a navy to fight Octavius in the Mediterranean. However, Cleopatra's ship flees at a moment of danger and Antony's forces are defeated. Antony is furious with Cleopatra, thinking that she plans to double-cross him, but he can't resist her. When he forgives her, Enobarbus knows that his master is finished. He defects.

Battles continue and, after an initial success, Antony's forces are once again crushed when the Egyptian fleet abandons the fight. This time, Antony is convinced that he has been betrayed and vows to capture Cleopatra. She goes into hiding and sends word that she has committed suicide. Undone with grief, Antony stabs himself. He is carried to Cleopatra and they are briefly reunited before he dies. Octavius takes Cleopatra prisoner, planning to exhibit her in Rome to demonstrate the power of his empire. She elects to die with pride and uses poisonous snakes to take her own life.

The play is intensely theatrical. Stage designers relish the rapidly shifting contrast between the rigid, fascistic lines of Rome and the luscious, cushioned decadence of Egypt. It has sex, scandal, luxury, celebrity and spectacle, but above all it has Cleopatra. This is the only one of the Shakespeare plays where the tragedy belongs equally to the woman. Unlike Ophelia or Cordelia, she is not merely the collateral damage of a man's demise. She dies as she lived – in complete control of her image. She cannot tolerate the thought that if she is taken captive she will be drooled over by 'slaves in greasy aprons' and satirized by impersonators: 'Antony / Shall be brought drunken forth,

and I shall see / Some squeaking Cleopatra boy my greatness /
In the posture of a whore.'[1] 'To boy' refers to a young man act-
ing the part of a woman, which is precisely what happened on
Shakespeare's stage. It is the theatrical implication of the way
she will be remembered that grips Cleopatra at the moment of
her death and the dignity conferred on her by Shakespeare's
play is its own commentary. She got what she wanted.

Cleopatra is a disconcerting role model for women. There
is something of Queen Elizabeth I about her. Shakespeare's
patron died in 1603, three years before he wrote the play. Like
Cleopatra, she had maintained her mystique by scrupulously
manufacturing her image. But whereas Elizabeth invented her-
self as the Virgin Queen, stomached like a man and with an
unassailable heart, Cleopatra invents herself as an icon whose
feminine sexuality is both powerful and (to an Elizabethan
audience, at least) unsettling.

Where on earth are we going to look in the Bible for a role
model for women who is as compelling as that? Let's look in
Proverbs.

Who shall find a virtuous woman? for her price is far above
the pearls ...
She is like the ships of merchants: she bringeth her food
from afar.
And she ariseth, while it is yet night: and giveth the portion
to her household, and the ordinary to her maids.
She considereth a field, and getteth it: and with the fruit of
her hands she planteth a vineyard.
She girdeth her loins with strength, and strengtheneth her
arms ...
She stretcheth out her hand to the poor, and putteth forth
her hands to the needy ...
She maketh sheets, and selleth them, and giveth girdles unto
the merchant ...
She openeth her mouth with wisdom, and the law of grace
is in her tongue ...

---

1 Act 5, Scene 2.

Her children rise up, and call her blessed: her husband also
    shall praise her, saying,
Many daughters have done virtuously: but thou
    surmountest them all.
Favour is deceitful, and beauty is vanity: but a woman that
    feareth the Lord shall be praised.
Give her of the fruit of her hands, and let her own works
    praise her in the gates.[2]

That is a colossal list of expectations, and it is only part of the chapter. In all, the writer lists 22 qualities of a woman who is virtuous. It seems to suggest that to be godly and female you need to be Wonder Woman. Or at the very least, the Queen of Egypt. I find myself uncomfortable at that thought. There is something dispiriting about magazines which expect that every woman will have a thriving career while maintaining an immaculate home in which she overturns gender stereotypes by being the one who clears the gutters, meanwhile caring for perfect children, being endlessly creative in bed and staying up-to-date with the music that is playing at 3am in the night-clubs.

There is, however, another way of looking at it. It is no accident that there are 22 features. There are 22 letters in the Hebrew alphabet. This is not a checklist, but a poem, and each line of the poem begins with a different letter of the language in which it was written.

In that context, it is entirely positive that it rejects body image as a measure of worth ('beauty is vanity'). Instead it makes virtues of skill, work, wisdom, charity, community and faith. And the final line insists that none of these things are to be taken for granted; they are to be honoured ('let her own works praise her in the gates').

---

2 Proverbs 31.10, 14–17, 20, 24, 26, 28–31.

I like to have a touch of Enobarbus about the way I read
this chapter of Proverbs. It is not a list of expectations but a
glorious tribute to 22 ways in which a woman can be magnifi-
cent. It's an A–Z of thank-yous by a man to the women of the
world.

Day 30

Remembrance of things past

When to the sessions of sweet silent thought
I summon up remembrance of things past,
I sigh the lack of many a thing I sought,
And with old woes new wail my dear time's waste:
Then can I drown an eye, unused to flow,
For precious friends hid in death's dateless night,
And weep afresh love's long since cancelled woe,
And moan the expense of many a vanished sight:
Then can I grieve at grievances foregone,
And heavily from woe to woe tell o'er
The sad account of fore-bemoaned moan,
Which I new pay as if not paid before.
   But if the while I think on thee, dear friend,
   All losses are restored and sorrows end.

Sonnet 30

James I came to the throne of England in 1603, having already been King of Scotland for 20 years. There were many things for which he had an extravagant appetite: food (it was said that you could identify every meal he'd had since his coronation by the stains on his clothes), sex (he had a preference for the Gentlemen of the Bedchamber, but he also fathered seven children) and jewellery (the £47,000 he spent in 1604 would now be worth £6 million). But his biggest love was theatre. One of his first acts after becoming king was to grant Shakespeare's troupe a royal patent. They become The King's Men. No higher honour could have been possible. They performed for him about once a month.

William was now wealthy. Most of his money, though, seems to have been sent back to Stratford, where he purchased land. The lodgings in which he is known to have lived in London were modest.

Later in 1603, though, bubonic plague once again closed the London theatres. The King's Men went on tour for most of the year. At the end of the year, they performed *Hamlet* 15 miles up the River Thames at Hampton Court. The company was paid £103 by the king and given a £30 bonus because of their loss of income during the year. A year later, in the same room, James hosted the conference of theologians that would result in a new translation of the Bible being published in 1611 – the Authorized Version (or King James Version). James had a strong dislike of the Geneva Bible (from which the quotations in this book have been taken). The problem was not the text but the footnotes and comments on nearly every verse. In them, monarchs are called 'tyrants' and the theology is sympathetic to Puritanism, with the need for a church hierarchy being questioned.

The theatres reopened in 1604 and plans began to build a new theatre. The Blackfriars Theatre was an indoor venue and it seated about 600. This introduced a new range of possibilities. It was candle-lit. The entire audience was closer, offering new subtleties for the acting and stage business. There were special effects and scenery changes. The musicians could use strings instead of trumpets.

The new theatre opened in 1608. With the cheapest seats costing six pence instead of the one penny that was charged for admission to the Globe, it attracted a different crowd. And that had a significant impact on the profits, which must have pleased Shakespeare, who had a one-sixth interest in the business. The following year, on 20 May, a slim volume called *Shakespeare's Sonnets Never Before Imprinted* went on sale.

There are no clues as to when the 154 poems in the volume were written. Most scholars associate them with the early part of Shakespeare's life, because there is a youthful energy about the love they describe. However, it's possible that he returned to writing poetry again and again, especially when contagion closed the theatres. And today's sonnet, number 30, has a sense of someone in later years looking back on his life and sighing.

You can hear the sighs. If you read the first line aloud, with all those words beginning with the letter S, you will actually sigh in the process. It's what the poet does when he sits in 'sweet, silent thought' and looks back on his life. He then uses a direct quotation from the Bible. It comes from a book called The Wisdom of Solomon in the Old Testament Apocrypha: 'A double grief came upon them, and a groaning for the remembrance of things past.'[1] (It refers to the lament of the Egyptians after the Hebrew people had escaped slavery.)

The poet's grief, though, is more than double. In his past there has been 'many a thing I sought' which came to nothing. There were 'precious friends' who have died young. Heartbreaks caused by love, even the hurts that are 'long since cancelled', return as if they have never gone away. Each one is a 'fore-bemoaned moan' because he has lamented it many times in the past. But he pays the price of them all over again, as if the pain is brand new. And, oh, all the wasted time!

The structure is one that is typical of the sonnets. There are three quatrains with a steady pattern of rhymes and half-rhymes and then the mood changes completely in the closing couplet. Thinking about a particular friend completely changes the circumstances. The certain knowledge of his love means that everything the poet thought he had lost is given back. 'Sorrows end.'

The straightforwardness of those last two lines, with their effortless rhythm and emphatic rhyme, suggest that there's no doubt about it. He is snapped out of those brooding memories by an acute metaphor. 'All losses are restored' is a figure of speech from the world of financial accounting. There are several of them in the final few lines: 'tell o'er … account … paid'. He is filing his losses and profits like a tax return. There's nothing like a bit of book-keeping to replace spirit-sapping emotions with positive thoughts.

---

1 Wisdom of Solomon 11.12.

You can insure yourself against money being stolen from you. But it's impossible to insure yourself against time being stolen from you. We all look back, as the poet does, and feel sadness for what is no more. More than sadness; it's a kind of grief.

In the Old Testament, the book of Joel describes those seasons that have been stolen from us as locust years. Locust years are fruitless years in which we invest energy and emotion in projects that come to nothing. In Joel's day it was literal – a crop that had been sown and nurtured with great care was devastated by a plague of locusts.[2] But for us it could be a failed venture or a relationship that didn't last. All that effort and what have I got to show for it?

Locust years are painful years. They may involve the death of someone significant, taking with them plans you had for the future. Or maybe an illness robs you of things that you assumed you would always be able to do.

Locust years are loveless years. Affection drains out of a marriage, or a family division leaves you lost and alone. Or perhaps a rebellious past which once seemed like an adventure now seems like a dead end. Why did I make that decision? Why didn't I take that opportunity?

Hear the words of the Lord as Joel recorded them, full of the promise of restoration and hope. In the magnificent translation of the Geneva Bible, it is not merely locusts, but:

I will repay you the years that the grasshopper hath eaten,
the cankerworm and the caterpillar and the palmerworm,
my great host which I sent among you.
So you shall eat and be satisfied and praise the name of the
    Lord your God,
that hath dealt marvellously with you.[3]

---

2 Joel 1.2–4.
3 Joel 2.25, 26.

How does God repay us in those circumstances? He is a God for whom nothing need ever be wasted. He is a recycling God. There is always something that he wants us to learn. If we allow him to he can recycle our mistakes, even the ones we regret deeply, to produce wisdom that enriches our lives. He can recycle our failures to generate advice for our friends. He can recycle sadness to produce sympathy for others. He can recycle an understanding of what it means to be in need to produce generosity. Experiences are repurposed on and on through our lives until, in the goodness of God, death recycles us into his presence – that place where 'all losses are restored and sorrows end'.

The Bible urges us not to succumb to the listless ache of regret, but to look instead to the future: 'Remember ye not the former things, neither regard the things of old. Behold, I do a new thing: now shall it come forth.'[4] Isaiah attributes these words to God and addresses them to the Jews. There was a reason why they were able to do this and it speaks to us with life-changing reassurance down the centuries:

> When thou passest through the waters, I will be with thee,
> and through the floods, that they do not overflow thee ...
> Because thou wast precious in my sight, and thou wast
>   honourable, and I loved thee.[5]

So it turns out to be about love after all. It probably doesn't turn the situation around as quickly and effortlessly as it does in Shakespeare's sonnet, but it is steadfast and has sustained countless generations of God's people in their times of regret. May it sustain you too in the heart of Lent.

---

4 Isaiah 43.18.
5 Isaiah 43.2, 4.

Day 31

O beware, my Lord, of jealousy; it is the green-eyed monster

OTHELLO: By heaven, I'll know thy thoughts.
IAGO: You cannot, if my heart were in your hand;
Nor shall not, whilst 'tis in my custody.
OTHELLO: Ha!
IAGO: O, beware, my lord, of jealousy;
It is the green-eyed monster which doth mock
The meat it feeds on; that cuckold lives in bliss
Who, certain of his fate, loves not his wronger;
But, O, what damned minutes tells he o'er
Who dotes, yet doubts, suspects, yet strongly loves!
OTHELLO: O misery!
IAGO: Poor and content is rich and rich enough,
But riches fineless is as poor as winter
To him that ever fears he shall be poor.
Good heaven, the souls of all my tribe defend
From jealousy!

Othello, Act 3, Scene 3

Although it's not possible to be sure, I think Othello is a convert from Islam to Christianity. He uses the phrase 'By heaven' often, as he does here, and elsewhere he speaks of grace. One of the other characters mentions the fact that he has been baptized and he urges his wife to pray. Shakespeare describes him as a moor, which might mean that he is a Muslim or that he comes from North Africa. Either way, he is a black man who has made a success of his life as a soldier, but is never made to feel that he fits in a privileged white society.

Some productions make much of Othello's religion; others less.[1] One of the white characters accuses Othello of having used witchcraft and 'foul charms' to persuade his daughter to marry him, which is uncomfortable to read if it is a reference to Othello's former faith. The daughter, Desdemona, refutes this. She married for love.

However, no production can ignore the implications of Othello's race. The role was originally played by an actor called Richard Burbage, who also played Lear, Macbeth and other leading roles. We know from descriptions of other sixteenth-century entertainments that he would have played the part in dark face paint and a curly wig. For a white actor to use make-up in order to play the role of a black hero would be unthinkable in the twenty-first century.

Racism as we know it today is very different from the circumstances that Shakespeare would have known. The enslavement of African people for the transatlantic slave trade was still in its infancy. People of colour owned property in London and there were mixed-race marriages. Scholars of the time thought the colour of African skin was caused by exposure to the sun, or that it was related somehow to a curse that Noah put on one of his sons, Ham.

Othello's downfall comes about because Iago, one of his soldiers, becomes obsessed with destroying him. It is never made absolutely clear what Iago's motivation is. He is certainly bitter because he has been passed over for the role of Othello's lieutenant. He seems to think, with or without justification, that Othello has slept with his wife. But none of these fully account for the determination with which he revels in plotting the general's death. And into that gap that Shakespeare has left, racism creeps and colours each production in a new way.

Iago has a quality that is invaluable as he manipulates people. They trust him. First, he manipulates a rich man called Roderigo, who is paying him to help woo Desdemona. It's too late, it transpires, because she has wed Othello. Then he

---

1 In Stuart Burge's 1965 film, Othello rips the cross he has been wearing from his neck as his thoughts turn murderous.

observes Cassio, the man who gained the promotion he thought should have been his, offering Desdemona a gentlemanly hand. He tells the audience that he will use that gesture to sow the thought in Othello's mind that they might be lovers and allow jealousy to take hold.

He contrives a fight between Roderigo and Cassio, and Cassio is stripped of his post as lieutenant. Iago persuades Cassio that the best way back into Othello's favour is to ask Desdemona to take his side. When Othello misconstrues something he observes between Cassio and Desdemona, Iago insists to Othello that he has no reason to be jealous (today's speech). The more he protests friendship, the more damage he does. He persuades his wife Emilia to steal a handkerchief that was Othello's first gift to Desdemona and he hides it in Cassio's bedroom. When it is found it seems like irrefutable evidence. Iago arranges for Othello to overhear a conversation with Cassio about a relationship with a woman and he completely misinterprets it as being about his wife. His jealousy seethes.

In the catastrophe that follows, Othello kills Desdemona. In an effort to cover up what he has done, Iago murders several people, including his own wife. When the truth becomes clear, Othello is overcome with grief. He makes a speech of great beauty in which he explains that it was the depth of his love for Desdemona that caused the jealousy he now realizes was misplaced. He asks to be remembered as 'one who loved not wisely but too well'.[2] He has a concealed dagger and dies next to his wife. Iago surveys the wreckage he has caused and, awaiting justice, declares that he has nothing more to say.

We weep for Othello once he realizes that he 'threw a pearl away'. We loathe Iago, but Shakespeare gives him jokes and great speeches which force us into an awkward appreciation of the way his wickedness is so uncompromising. And so ingenious! Describing jealousy as 'the green-eyed monster' which not only devours a person but mocks him as he eats is savagely memorable. It is significant that the monster's eyes are green. In the biology of the day there were four fluids in the

---

2 Act 5, Scene 2.

body which needed to be in equilibrium for a person to have a balanced temperament. Green was the colour of bile, an indication of fear or envy.

Iago makes the case that suspicion that the wife you adore might be having an affair with someone you know is worse than the certainty of adultery with a stranger ('that cuckold lives in bliss'). Even if your riches are infinite ('fineless'), they are worthless if you fear they might be taken away. Such persuasiveness; such garbage!

Every plea to Othello to beware jealousy serves to increase it. And every lie further convinces him that the man who will wreck him is motivated by friendship. Iago knows that Othello is now as much in thrall to this narrative of disinformation as he is to the Bible: 'Trifles light as air / Are to the jealous confirmations strong / As proofs of holy writ.'[3]

Jealousy is deplored both in the Quran of the faith that Othello was born into and the Bible of the faith to which he has converted. In the Muslim scriptures: 'I seek refuge in the Lord of the daybreak from the evil … of an envier when he envies.'[4] In the Hebrew and Christian scriptures: 'Jealousy is the rage of a man: therefore he will not spare in the day of vengeance.'[5] And all three religions share the story of Cain, who killed his brother Abel out of jealousy. That story is mentioned in Shakespeare more often than any other Bible narrative – it appears 25 times in the 38 plays.

In the Bible, jealousy always involves three people or groups. It usually involves someone being displaced as the most important person in the life of someone they love. In the Old Testament, King Saul develops a rage against his army general David – a man who he himself had promoted. As war against their Philistine enemies generates one victory after another, women come out of the towns to greet them with celebratory dances, singing, 'Saul hath slain his thousand, and David his

---

3 Act 3, Scene 3.
4 Surah Al-Falaq 113:1, 5.
5 Proverbs 6.34.

ten thousand.'⁶ His jealousy over their relative popularity with their fans turns murderous, but David escapes.

Rachel becomes jealous of her sister Leah – both married to Jacob. Leah is bearing him children, but Rachel isn't. It rankles into a rivalry that involves competition for his affection, fertility drugs (mandrakes) and the use of slave girls as surrogates. Leah's life is a sad one, because Rachel is evidently Jacob's favourite and he is only married to Leah because of a deception. After Rachel dies, Jacob transfers his affection not to Leah but to her slave girl, Bilhah. The unhappiness blights the whole family.⁷ The sons born to the women copy the behaviour they observe. They grow up with such jealousy of their brother Joseph, also picked out by Jacob as his favourite, that they sell him to slave traders.

How then can God be described on many occasions as a jealous God? 'Take heed … lest ye make you any graven image, or likeness of anything, as the Lord thy God hath charged thee. For the Lord thy God is a consuming fire, and a jealous God.'⁸ This too is a relationship of three. God's love for his people is so blazingly intense that he cannot bear the thought that they might be unfaithful to him and pray to idols. They were meant for him only, as faithful and devoted as he is to them. When his people seek other ways to fulfil themselves, his jealousy burns as his heart breaks.

Jealousy progresses from loving to having, then from losing to hating. Envy is different. There are only two people involved in envy. It is a matter of hating and never having. Iago's failure is envy. Cassio has the promotion he wants and because of that he loathes him. Othello's failure is jealousy. He loves so fiercely that he loses everything. That is why we give our hearts to Othello and not to Iago.

As Christians, we are often invited to consider the immensity of God's love, but it is rare to be asked to think of that love as incorporating an immense jealousy. God is jealous of every

---

6 I Samuel 18.7.
7 Genesis 30.
8 Deuteronomy 4.23, 24.

moment we dally with ideas and behaviours that exclude him from our lives. He is jealous of money when we momentarily believe it can buy us a satisfaction that we cannot find in him. He is jealous of our nation when patriotism elevates a selfish love above a desire for all the people in his world to thrive. He is jealous of status when we think our dignity lies in achievement rather than service. He is jealous of comfort when we choose a path that evades any of the challenges, embarrassments or sacrifices that Jesus told his followers to expect.

The transformative truth to which Christians hold fast is that, as a consequence of that yearning jealousy, God chose not to take but to give. 'Herein was that love of God made manifest amongst us, because God sent his only begotten Son into this world, that we might live through him. Herein is that love, not that we loved God, but that he loved us.'[9] The very quality that might have dealt tragedy to humankind has instead brought us life. Extraordinary though it is to come to this conclusion, let us thank God for his jealousy. It has become our salvation.

---

9 1 John 4.9, 10.

Day 32

When in disgrace with fortune and men's eyes

When in disgrace with fortune and men's eyes
I all alone beweep my outcast state,
And trouble deaf heav'n with my bootless cries,
And look upon myself, and curse my fate,
Wishing me like to one more rich in hope,
Featured like him, like him with friends possessed,
Desiring this man's art, and that man's scope,
With what I most enjoy contented least;
Yet in these thoughts myself almost despising,
Haply I think on thee, and then my state,
Like to the lark at break of day arising
From sullen earth, sings hymns at heaven's gate.
　For thy sweet love remembered such wealth brings
　That then I scorn to change my state with kings.

Sonnet 29

Psalm 88 is the bleakest song in the Bible. It begins: 'O Lord
God of my salvation, I cry day and night before thee.'[1] That is
not so surprising. Several psalms begin by calling out to God
in a time of deep distress.
　It continues:

Unto thee have I cried, O Lord, and early shall my prayer
　come before thee.

---

1 Psalm 88.1.

Lord, why dost thou reject my soul, and hidest thy face
from me? ...
My lovers and friends hast thou put away from me.[2]

It is not so surprising to find those words in the Bible either.
Other psalms come from a place of agonized loneliness. They
speak of times when God is silent, 'hides his face' and does
nothing to help, even when prayers are repeated with increas-
ing desperation.

The thing that makes Psalm 88 unique is that nothing hap-
pens to turn the situation around. Unlike all the other psalms
which show their writers in torment, no hope is offered from
earth or heaven. God's silence persists. The writer of the psalm
ends in as desolate a condition as he was at the beginning.
Modern translations render the last line as: 'Darkness is my
closest friend.'[3]

This psalm is extremely precious to me. Others who have
experienced periods of ill health or misfortune have said the
same. There was a time some years ago when for several weeks
it was the only passage of the Bible I could read. Anything else
seemed too glib to contemplate. Bringing to mind God's great
deeds of salvation was impossible. However, it brought relief
to find permission deep in the Old Testament to pour grief out
to God without any requirement to pull myself together and
trust that all would be well that ends well.

The sonnet we are looking at today bears remarkable simi-
larities with that anguished psalm. The poet is out of luck,
out of favour and out of friends. He is alone and in tears
('beweep my outcast state'). He has tried to pray but there is
no response. God might as well be deaf ('trouble deaf heav'n
with my bootless cries' – bootless means of no use whatsoever).
When he curses his fate, he may be trying to make us think of
Job who, in the Old Testament, lost family, fortune and health
and 'opened his mouth and cursed his day'.[4]

---

2 Psalm 88.4, 13, 14, 18.
3 Psalm 88.18 (NIV).
4 Job 3.1.

He is also aware of his own inadequacy compared with those around him who have hope, good looks ('featured'), talent or opportunity ('scope'). He has lost interest in all the things which used to give him pleasure. The first eight lines have unwavering rhymes to match their unremitting gloom. So far so Psalm 88.

But there is a but. As in many other Shakespeare sonnets, the first eight lines set up a premise and the last six respond in a different way altogether. The poem turns on the word 'yet'. The writer has one thing that allows him to rise from his depression. He has a love in his life. That love alone is able to make existence worthwhile. The very thought of it can relieve his wretchedness. In fact, it can do more than relieve it; it can transform his whole demeanour. Unlike the psalm, the sonnet ends in joy. The poet would rather have his problems and keep his lover than have all the glory of royalty without her. Or him. ('I scorn to change my state with kings.')

The closing lines of the poem are as exhilarating as a lark ascending. The way Shakespeare achieves this is by choosing words with soft consonants and alliteration (like and lark, hymns and heaven – you can actually hear his spirits lifting). They too call on Christian imagery – a chorus of praise. No longer is God estranged. He was once deaf, but now he hears. The poet's soul is restored. The final couplet, with its ringing rhymes, brings a settled certainty to the close of the poem. Love has brought liberation.

Who was this person who had so wonderfully lifted the poet's gloom? There are two schools of thought about whether the sonnets should be read in an autobiographical way or as the work of a poet putting himself in someone else's shoes. The first group tries to identify a stage in Shakespeare's life at which he was brought low and then to pinpoint the man or woman who might have given him solace. The reason for writing 'man or woman' is that many of the poems are addressed to a 'fair youth' who is indisputably male. (There are some saucy puns about the male anatomy in various sonnets to prove it.) The second group points out that poets as magnificent as Shakespeare don't only write from their own experience, but from a rich imagination. He didn't, after all, need to have attempted suicide in order to write the 'To be or not to be' speech from *Hamlet* with such insight.

So we don't know. There are, however, some clues. Shakespeare had taken the fancy of Henry Wriothesley, the third Earl of Southampton. I use the word 'fancy' advisedly. Henry loved a good fight and married in his mid-twenties, but he was also as camp as a dandy. When they were both relatively young, he became Shakespeare's patron. What else he became is anybody's guess, despite many people attempting to infer a gay relationship. However, his support made Shakespeare rich.

When Shakespeare published his sonnets in 1609, full of love and longing, he dedicated the book to Mr WH. The dedication described him as their 'only begetter' (sole inspiration). There are several theories about who that could be, but it's tempting to think they were a personal message to Henry Wriothesley, disguised by swapping the initials.

Is it Mr WH who made the poet's heart soar? Or are those the kinds of words anyone would use in order to flatter a patron in the hope of generosity? Or is this a poet's creativity rising above autobiography?

It's all gorgeous and uplifting. But the ease of Sonnet 29, where love is all it takes to lift depression, doesn't have the ring of truth that the Bible has about where comfort is going to be found in a time of mental ill health.

There is a choice to be made today. Do you want to carry Psalm 88 or Sonnet 29 with you through the final week of Lent? Many people will choose the Shakespeare poem because it is easy to identify with the turmoil of the beginning of the poem, but then the beautiful turnaround of the last six lines is rich with optimism.

Personally, I am going to choose the bleak reality of Psalm 88. Its uncompromising honesty is a strange comfort. All those centuries ago, someone found room for this in the Bible. They made a decision not to offer an easy hope that depression will be resolved by the discovery of an idealized friend or lover.

They didn't give an expectation that God would make himself known in a flood of peace and healing.

Instead they offered a way to bring our hopelessness to God, knowing that because these words are in the heart of the Bible it is in every way acceptable to hurt and howl in this way. There is no guarantee of a Henry Wriothesley, nor of a 'hymn at heaven's gate'. But equally, there is no thought too outrageous to bring to God. And that is a great consolation.

Day 33

There is a world elsewhere

CORIOLANUS: You common cry of curs! whose breath I hate
As reek o' the rotten fens, whose loves I prize
As the dead carcasses of unburied men
That do corrupt my air, I banish you;
And here remain with your uncertainty!
Let every feeble rumour shake your hearts!
Your enemies, with nodding of their plumes,
Fan you into despair! Have the power still
To banish your defenders; till at length
Your ignorance, which finds not till it feels,
Making not reservation of yourselves,
Still your own foes, deliver you as most
Abated captives to some nation
That won you without blows! Despising,
For you, the city, thus I turn my back:
There is a world elsewhere.

Coriolanus, Act 3, Scene 3

Coriolanus is the story of a right-wing politician in a time of poverty and hunger, who despises the people he wants to govern but needs their votes. It is set in Rome about five centuries before Jesus. For reasons that will become clear, it is often performed in modern dress.

At the start of the play, Coriolanus is a war hero. He returns to Rome after defeating a neighbouring tribe, the Volscians, and their leader Aufidius. The Senate plans to make him a consul. However, the workers who supply Rome with its food must endorse the appointment and he must follow tradition by appearing before them. He is expected to dress plainly and plead humbly for their approval. This is loathsome to a proud, compassionless man like Coriolanus, but needs must. He makes an appearance in front of the 'mutable, rank-scented' commoners.

Initially they laud him. But then they are persuaded by their leaders that he is 'an enemy to the people', because he is complicit with the circumstances that have left them impoverished, and they reject him. They seek to have him banished. Coriolanus is livid and his response is today's speech.

He doesn't hold back. They are all dogs ('curs'). Their breath stinks. He needs their love no more than he needs the love of a carcass. It's not a case of being expelled by them; rather, he chooses to banish Rome. He hopes there will be so many rumours of invading enemies that they will live in constant fear and despair. He hopes they will banish every single leader who would have defended them so that they are eventually overrun by some nation 'without blows' because they are too feeble to lift any weapons. He turns his back on them and leaves the city. You can hear the spittle of his scorn in every line until he declares that he is better off without them: 'There is a world elsewhere.'

With his heart set on revenge, Coriolanus goes to Aufidius of the Volscians. He makes peace with his old enemy. Together they plan an assault on Rome and the city seems helpless to stop the advance. Two of his old friends visit him, encamped outside the city, and plead for mercy. He rebuffs them. But then his mother Volumnia, whom he adores, goes to him and pleads for mercy. In a tense and touching scene, she sinks to her knees before him. He relents. Volumnia returns to be hailed as Rome's saviour. But Coriolanus' concession to his mother is his undoing. Aufidius feels betrayed and, in the row that follows, Coriolanus is murdered.

This play is not performed as often as other Shakespeare plays that are set in Rome, but it is politically fascinating. In recent years it has been performed increasingly often across the world because its themes chime with the political experience of various countries. Do our leaders seek power to further their own ambitions or because they have a vision for improving the lot of those who are most vulnerable? Can politicians who espouse the populism that juxtaposes the people against the elite provide a solution to inequality, or are they part of the problem? Will a nation be judged by its compassion or by its strength?

The language doesn't have the rich musicality of other plays, but it has memorable images. Coriolanus' friend Menenius tells Volumnia that her son has 27 battle scars and 'every gash was an enemy's grave'. (You can hear the thrust of a weapon in the rhythm and the alliteration.) With death approaching, he describes his war record as 'like an eagle in a dove-cote'.

It's not easy to like a hero who is so proud and disdainful of the poor. But there is something noble about his refusal to pretend to be anything other than his stubbornly aristocratic self in order to win acclaim. And there are moments, particularly in his relationship with his wife and his mother, when we glimpse the kind of man he could have been. It is his uncharacteristic decision to show mercy that brings about his downfall.

There are superb details which show the virtues trapped within Coriolanus that cannot find expression. For instance, when he arrives home victorious against the Volscians, he reveals that among the prisoners of war he has noticed a man who, although poor, had given him hospitality. He wants the man to be released in recognition of the kindness he showed towards an adversary. But then he can't remember the man's name so nothing can be done for him. The man presumably goes off to his death and Coriolanus puts it out of his mind and calls for wine.

Coriolanus doesn't have a soliloquy that allows the audience to understand, and maybe sympathize with, the inner turmoil that leads him to betray his city. We are left to infer them from the scene, crackling with drama, from which today's speech comes. As the tension mounts, we watch accusations being thrown at Coriolanus, knowing that they are jabbing at his rawest wounds and that one of them will make him snap.

When he is called a traitor, he summons the fires of hell to incinerate his opponents: 'The fires i' the lowest hell fold-in the people!'

All this makes an intriguing comparison with two monumental showdowns that take place in the Bible. The first took place in Samaria two centuries before the time of the real-life Coriolanus. 2 Kings tells us that King Ahaziah fell from an upstairs gallery in his palace. Desperate to know whether he was going to survive his injuries, he sent a delegation to the shrine of the god Baal in order to get a divination. On the way, they met a man with wild hair, clothes woven from a camel's mane and a leather belt.[1] He furiously lambasted them for visiting a worthless idol instead of seeking answers from the true God and sent them back with the message that the king should get ready for death.

When they reported this to the king, he asked them what the man had looked like. They described him and Ahaziah groaned, 'Oh gods help us! That was Elijah, you idiots.' He sent 50 soldiers to seek out Elijah and summon him to the palace. They found him sitting at the top of a hill and there was a stand-off. They shouted their commands up at him. Elijah called down fire from heaven which incinerated them.

On hearing the news, Ahaziah sent a further group of 50 soldiers. When they reached Elijah, they too tried to arrest him and bring him to the palace. Ill-advisedly! Fire fell from the sky and burnt them up.

A third group of soldiers took a more considered approach. Their captain ascended the hill and sank to his knees in front of the man of God. He pleaded with Elijah to have respect for his life and made his request. This time Elijah consented and went with the delegation. He gave the bad news to King Ahaziah in person, who never left his bed again.

The other Bible story took place in the very same location, but is a total contrast. Jesus was travelling from Galilee to Jerusalem, knowing that death lay ahead of him. He took

---

1 2 Kings 1.1–17. The Geneva Bible draws attention to the hair. Later translations focus on the clothes.

the route that was most direct, although not the most stress-free because it involved passing through Samaria. There was a longstanding animosity between Jews and Samaritans, who had inter-married with other tribes, rejected parts of the Jewish Scriptures and did not recognize Jerusalem as the focus of their worship of God.

Looking for a place to stay, Jesus sent a message to a Samaritan village. When they heard that he and his companions were bound for Jerusalem, they refused to let him in. The villagers were rejecting Jesus in the same way that Elijah had been insulted many centuries before. James and John must have known since their earliest days the story of fire being summoned to destroy churlish opponents. They were outraged on behalf of their friend Jesus, dismissing the Samaritans as a half-caste tribe who had no idea of the significance of the man at their gates. They expected a Coriolanus-like eruption. Surely it was time for another inferno. They were ready to invoke the flames without delay.[2]

Jesus too was furious. However, his anger wasn't directed at the Samaritan village, but at his own disciples. Revenge had no place in his plan for humankind. Instead, Jesus turned his face towards a different hill. There he would submit to violence without resisting in pursuit of the peace of the entire human race. There was a world elsewhere.

---

2 Luke 9.51–56.

Day 34

Friends, Romans, countrymen, lend me your ears

MARK ANTONY:
Friends, Romans, countrymen, lend me your ears;
I come to bury Caesar, not to praise him.
The evil that men do lives after them;
The good is oft interred with their bones;
So let it be with Caesar. The noble Brutus
Hath told you Caesar was ambitious:
If it were so, it was a grievous fault,
And grievously hath Caesar answered it.
Here, under leave of Brutus and the rest –
For Brutus is an honourable man;
So are they all, all honourable men –
Come I to speak in Caesar's funeral.
He was my friend, faithful and just to me:
But Brutus says he was ambitious;
And Brutus is an honourable man.
He hath brought many captives home to Rome
Whose ransoms did the general coffers fill:
Did this in Caesar seem ambitious?
When that the poor have cried, Caesar hath wept:
Ambition should be made of sterner stuff:
Yet Brutus says he was ambitious;
And Brutus is an honourable man.

Julius Caesar, Act 3, Scene 2

How do you stand up to a tyrant?
This is The Tragedy With the Wrong Title. One-third of the
way through, Julius Caesar is murdered by conspirators who

think he is going to become a tyrant. The play is actually about how Brutus, Caesar's trusted friend, is persuaded that the only way to save Rome, the city he loves, is to kill him. It is the wrong decision. It's the calamity that comes upon him subsequently that fires the play.

As it begins, the politician and army general Julius Caesar has defeated his rival in battle and is preparing for a victory parade through Rome. A psychic shouts that he should 'beware the Ides of March' (15 March was a religious festival devoted to the god Jupiter).[1] Caesar ignores him.

Brutus talks to Cassius, another colleague of Caesar. Their fear is that Caesar is being treated by the crowds as if he were a god and that he will proclaim himself king, bringing democracy in the Roman Republic to an end. Meanwhile, Caesar's closest ally, Antony, makes a public spectacle of offering Caesar the crown, but he refuses it.

That night, Rome is struck by terrible weather and portents of disaster. Under cover of darkness, Cassius plants fake letters for Brutus to find which seem to suggest that the public believes Caesar has too much power. Brutus is driven by a devotion to Rome; Cassius by scheming ambition. But the letters are sufficient to win Brutus over to the assassination plot.

The ides of March come and, despite his wife's nightmares and further warnings, Caesar goes to the senate. One by one the conspirators stab him and, when he sees that his friend Brutus is among them, he gives up the struggle: 'Et tu Brute! Then fall, Caesar.'[2]

At Caesar's funeral, Brutus makes a speech proclaiming that although he loved Caesar, he loves Rome more. The tyrant had to die. And then Antony takes the stand and makes the brilliant speech on which we are focused today. The entire direction of the play changes.

The speech appears to be deferential to the conspirators, but line by line it becomes more subversive. It begins with impeccable politeness in the famous and much-parodied request for

---

1 Act 1, Scene 2.
2 Act 3, Scene 1.

'friends, Romans, countrymen' to listen. He states that he has come to tell them about the evil that Caesar did, fatally ambitious to laud it over them as a despotic king. He is sure that this must be correct because it's what Brutus has told them, and 'Brutus is an honourable man.' That line comes back again and again. Each time Antony suggests that Caesar was ambitious it seems less blameworthy. He was ambitious to defeat their enemies and bring 'many captives home to Rome'. He was ambitious to alleviate suffering and so empathetic that 'when that the poor have cried, Caesar hath wept'. In contrast, each time he declares that Brutus is honourable it sounds more sarcastic.

The crowd is won over. When Antony goes on to read Caesar's will and reveals that he has left a sum of money to every citizen, they are enraged by the injustice of his death and turn against the assassins.

In a setting in which fate is unstoppable and supernatural forces have power, it is inevitable that Caesar's ghost will 'cry "Havoc" and let slip the dogs of war'.[3] Antony's army advances on the troops of Cassius and Brutus. Cassius sees his men fleeing and hears that Brutus' army is floundering. In despair that his ambitions are coming to nothing, he kills himself. Brutus suffers a further defeat in battle and, hearing of Cassius' death, kills himself as well. Antony declares him 'the noblest Roman of them all'[4] because while the others were schemers, he genuinely wanted what was best for their city. He saved it from a tyrant but, oh, at what a cost.

Some 75 years later, Jesus lived under tyranny. The Roman emperor had appointed Pontius Pilate to be the governor of the province in which Jerusalem was located. What kind of man was he? A brutal sadist who used terror to maintain his authority. While Jews were making sacrifices in the temple, he had them murdered so that their blood was mingled with the

---

3 Act 3, Scene 1.
4 Act 5, Scene 5.

blood of the animals they were offering to God.[5] Even by the standards of the time that was disgusting.

The Roman army had military standards on which the figure of the Emperor Tiberius was embossed. The Jews found this highly offensive because Roman emperors declared themselves to be gods. There was a longstanding agreement that these images would not be brought into Jerusalem, so close to the temple where Jews worshipped the one God in whom they believed. All Pilate's predecessors had respected this. But they didn't have the bloody-minded temperament of Pilate. He knew there would be trouble. So he had the standards smuggled in under cover of night. It led to a stand-off at his summer palace in Caesarea, 50 miles away on the coast. For five days, a group of Jewish men knelt around his house and bared their necks, willing to accept martyrdom rather than live with this blasphemy. Pilate relented, but it served to escalate the acrimony between him and the Jews.

Knowing he had to keep a lid on trouble, Pilate rode into Jerusalem in advance of the Jewish festival of Passover. Jews believed that when God sent them the Messiah who would overthrow their enemies, it would be during that festival. With thousands of Jews in the city to celebrate Passover, tensions were high.

Travelling from Caesarea, Pilate would have come from the west. Without doubt he would have ridden a magnificent horse and been flanked by soldiers. You can imagine him advancing, rigid and imperious.

Shortly afterwards, Jesus came to Jerusalem for the Passover. We know from Luke's Gospel that he came from the east, the opposite of Pilate's route.[6] And he wasn't riding a magnificent horse; he was riding a donkey.

The crowds recognized precisely what was going on. It was a huge mickey-take. What a laugh! They ripped down branches from the trees and waved them joyfully – teasing the donkey, loving the miracle-worker, dancing with the daring of it all.

---

5 Luke 13.1.
6 Luke 19.37.

But Luke's Gospel draws attention to Jesus' face. Tears were streaming down his cheeks. The truth that the crowd had been trying to escape overwhelmed him. They were in a city broken with suffering. It was a city that needed salvation.[7]

Someone yelled, 'Blessed be the king that cometh in the name of the Lord!' That was a bold move, because it comes from a psalm that was associated with the coming of the victorious Messiah.[8] The cry was taken up.

Jesus was calculatedly forcing them to a crunch point. This was the day when they had to decide. Are you for me, or are you for Pilate? Are you for a kingdom where the poor hear good news and the oppressed go free, or are you for an empire where the vulnerable are exploited and a distant emperor rules the country through a rich elite? The way of the donkey or the way of the charger?

So what were they going to do? In fact, they did something ancient, but full of meaning. They performed a ritual from Jerusalem's golden age when kings had been proclaimed. They took off their cloaks and flung them under Jesus' feet on the path ahead of him and the donkey trampled on them.[9] It was a sign of submission. My only cloak under my only leader. Long live the king!

Jesus was making powerful enemies. However, because the crowd on his side was huge, the authorities found it difficult to stop him. Jesus knew all this. He knew the power of peaceful protest. But he also knew how much that could cost. It might mean him sacrificing everything. For the sake of a people broken with suffering, for the sake of a world that needed salvation, he made his way through the city gates and prepared for the week that would bring him face to face with Pilate.

How do you stand up to a tyrant?

---

7 Luke 19.41.
8 Luke 19.38, Psalm 118.
9 2 Kings 9.13.

Day 35

We will solicit heaven and move the gods to send down justice

TITUS: And, sith there's no justice in earth nor hell,
We will solicit heaven and move the gods
To send down Justice for to wreak our wrongs.
Come, to this gear. You are a good archer, Marcus;
(He gives them arrows.)
'Ad Jovem,' that's for you: here, 'Ad Apollinem:'
'Ad Martem,' that's for myself:
Here, boy, to Pallas: here, to Mercury:
To Saturn, Caius, not to Saturnine;
You were as good to shoot against the wind.
To it, boy! Marcus, loose when I bid.
Of my word, I have written to effect;
There's not a god left unsolicited.
(They shoot.)

Titus Andronicus, Act 4, Scene 3

Arrows are fired into the air during the speech you have just read. They are tipped with papers that detail the sins of the Emperor of Rome, Saturninus. Evil is going unpunished. There is no justice on earth, and hell has made matters worse. So Titus Andronicus is trying to send a message to the Roman gods in the sky – Jove (Jupiter), Apollo, Mars and Saturn. It is a prayer of a kind – more of an act of crazy desperation. Send down justice to avenge ('wreak') the wrongs that have been done to Titus' family!

It's a highly theatrical scene. Wrapped up in these actions are fear, rage and futility. And also irony, because the arrows actually fall in the courtyard of Saturninus' palace and, when he discovers them, the result is a wave of atrocities that engulfs all the characters.

It is one of a small number of memorable scenes from Shakespeare's least accomplished and most violent play, *Titus Andronicus*. It puts on stage rape, beheading, murder, mutilation, honour killing, live burial and cannibalism. There is a total of 23 monstrous crimes in the play. Twenty-four if you count the poetry.

This play was immensely popular at the end of the sixteenth century. It was written by a young and inexperienced playwright (William was in his mid-twenties) and it offered his audience precisely the low-brow entertainment that they craved. This was an audience, remember, who on the afternoons when plays were not performed would come back to the theatre to watch some wretched bear being torn apart by dogs.

The play then fell completely out of favour. A century later, one critic described it as 'rather a heap of Rubbish than a structure'.[1] For hundreds of years it went virtually unperformed. And then, after the Second World War, a new interest in the play emerged. Atrocities that had seemed so excessive that they were unwatchable now appeared to have something to say about the realities of the evil that twentieth-century human beings were capable of. Its base language found new champions. Several memorable productions in recent years have made it impossible to dismiss. The questions it asks about how to stop a cycle of violence are relevant, even if the play is hard to enjoy.

Titus Andronicus is an ageing and wearied war hero. Unlike Coriolanus, he is entirely fictional. He arrives in Rome victorious over the Goths, bringing with him their queen, Tamora, as a prisoner of war and the coffins of his sons, killed in battle. His insistence that Tamora's eldest son is sacrificed as an offering to his own dead sons unleashes the hatred that will undo them all.

---

1 The dramatist Edward Ravenscroft, who presented an adapted version.

The emperor Saturninus marries Tamora and she uses that position to plot revenge with her lover Aaron. (Aaron is one of the few characters in Shakespeare who is specified as being black, and references to his wickedness coming naturally to someone with a skin of that colour are extremely disturbing.) She frames Titus' sons for a crime and has them executed. She goads her own sons into raping Titus' daughter Lavinia and then cutting off her hands and tongue so that she cannot identify her attackers.

Titus' only surviving son, Lucius, is banished from Rome. He joins the Goths and leads an army against the city. Titus is not in his right mind and Tamora takes advantage of it by dressing up as the figure of Revenge. She persuades him to summon Lucius to a banquet so that the Goths can be attacked in his absence. But Titus has not fallen for her trick. He seizes her sons. He has them butchered and serves them to Tamora at the banquet, cooked in a pie. Many deaths follow in revenge. The play ends with Lucius almost alone on stage, with Aaron's baby and a handful of attendants. His last words speak of rebuilding the state, but the vicious executions he has just ordered leave the audience wondering whether any worthy values underpin his plans.

There have been attempts to suggest that Shakespeare was not the author of the play. They are mainly based on embarrassment that the language is so poor and the violence so repugnant. However, most people now assume that he wrote it, perhaps with a collaborator. Although the poetry has none of the richness of his later plays, there are themes that keep returning to give the play a pulse. When Aaron reveals his motivation, it's stirring in a way that is recognizable as the way a terrorist leader stirs his troops to brutality: 'Vengeance is in my heart, death in my hand, / Blood and revenge are hammering in my head.'[2]

The value that has most moral currency in the play is honour. In the perverse world Shakespeare has created, the

---

2 Act 2, Scene 3.

very idea of forgiveness is such a weakness that it shames a person's honour. When Tamora suggests slyly that Saturninus might achieve more through clemency he roars back: 'What madam! be dishonoured openly, / And basely put it up without revenge.' The desolation of the end of the play demonstrates what happens in circumstances where only vengeance satisfies.

'O daughter of Babel, worthy to be destroyed, blessed shall he be that rewardeth thee, as thou hast served us. Blessed shall he be that taketh and dasheth thy children against the stones.' Uncomfortably, this is not a quotation from *Titus Andronicus*, but from the Bible.[3] Psalm 137 is one of a number of psalms that call on a vengeful God not to be silent, but to pay back the enemies of the Jewish people with the same suffering and disgrace that they have inflicted.

Defeated, brutalized and dragged into exile in Babylon ('Babel'), the thoughts of the Jews turned to revenge. It is easy to condemn, of course. But hear the grief-stricken tears of those lines from the psalm. No one alive could have a baby snatched from their arms and murdered without having to deal with thoughts that wish ill upon the perpetrator. We will never be able to offer an alternative to revenge unless we understand how readily the urge eats into all human hearts.

The awkward question is this. Is there any moral distinction between the cry for revenge of the people of God ('O Lord God the avenger … Exalt thyself, O judge of the world, and render a reward to the proud')[4] and Titus' family shooting arrows towards the stars and screaming for the justice that had been denied them?

In the first chapters of the Bible, Cain, a murderer, is condemned to a life in which he will never settle, never be at peace. His greatest fear is that he will have no protection from those seeking to take his life in revenge. God declares that his safety is assured because if anyone kills Cain he will be avenged seven times over.

---

3 Psalm 137.8–9.
4 Psalm 94.1–2.

His descendant Lamech was wounded by a young man. In revenge for the injury he had received he killed the boy. He gloated to his wives about his power. If Cain was the kind of man for whom vengeance was sufficient seven times over, he was the kind of man who would mete out vengeance 77 times over.

When the laws of the Old Testament stipulated that punishment should be 'eye for eye, tooth for tooth',[5] they sound brutal to our understanding of justice, but they were actually designed to stop revenge escalating out of control, as it had done for Lamech.

Jesus taught a gospel in which the desire for vengeance was not only constrained; it was turned on its head. His disciple Peter approached him with a question couched in such a way that I imagine he was hoping for a compliment. If someone wrongs you, how often should you forgive him? Is as much as seven times appropriate for a follower of Jesus? Jesus replied, 'I tell you, not seven times, but seventy-seven times.'[6] It was a deliberate and absolute repudiation of the way of Lamech.

It is impossible to insist that someone forgives another person. It can only come from the heart. And it is very difficult to find the resources to forgive someone when the offences continue two, four, seven, 77 times. It might be the repeated mocking of an accent, or the thoughtless noise of a neighbour, or the favouritism of a parent for another child.

The age of social media has made revenge so easy. A slighted boyfriend can send humiliating sexual images of a girl to a hundred people in a moment. The appetite it gratifies is the same as watching Lavinia, mute and mutilated on a bare stage. An affronted colleague can spread rumours, or undermine efforts, or make someone eat their own words. It's as demeaning as eating those words in a pie.

We have to find a different way of dealing with those who affront us. As Easter approaches, we have to find a different

---

5 Exodus 21.24.
6 Matthew 18.22 (NIV).

way. Every single one of us has someone with whom we wish we could get even. If it takes something as excessive as *Titus Andronicus* to make us look at ourselves and ask what the way of Jesus means for our humdrum desire to settle scores, so be it.

Day 36

Ay, but to die and go we know not where

CLAUDIO: Death is a fearful thing.
ISABELLA: And shamed life a hateful.
CLAUDIO: Ay, but to die, and go we know not where;
To lie in cold obstruction and to rot;
This sensible warm motion to become
A kneaded clod; and the delighted spirit
To bathe in fiery floods, or to reside
In thrilling region of thick-ribbed ice;
To be imprisoned in the viewless winds,
And blown with restless violence round about
The pendent world; or to be worse than worst
Of those that lawless and incertain thought
Imagine howling: 'tis too horrible!
The weariest and most loathed worldly life
That age, ache, penury and imprisonment
Can lay on nature is a paradise
To what we fear of death.
ISABELLA: Alas, alas!

Measure for Measure, Act 3, Scene 1

When you die your heart will stop beating. One minute later your breathing will cease. Your body will stiffen with rigor mortis four hours later. It will take 24 hours for your body to cool to room temperature.

I didn't find this out from researching medical textbooks. I have never seen a dead body. I know it all from television.

Dramas in which pathologists outwit criminals through what they discover during an autopsy have become favourites. I have learnt the mechanics of death through entertainment. Murder mysteries dominate bestseller lists. In cinemas, good-looking teenagers die in hideous ways as members of the audience jolt in their seats. It would be easy to compare this with the way the execution of a criminal was staged as a compelling day out during Shakespeare's lifetime. But criminals refused to die attractively. Twenty-first-century recreational death is packaged in such a way that we can shiver without retching.

The statistics for the actual event have remained constant over the years. It is still one out of every one. Within about 70 years of learning the facts of life, all of us, willingly or not, learn the facts of death.

Our readiness to consider death goes in and out of fashion as generations succeed one another. For the most part we are eager to talk about sex but uncomfortable talking about death. Although I can't recall how we got on to the subject during a casual chat, I remember asking a neighbour what she thought would happen after she died. She replied, 'Well, I expect I'll go to eternal bliss, but I don't like thinking about depressing things like that.'

Claudio, in *Measure for Measure*, in a prison cell where he is due to be executed, is not so much depressed as terrified. He fears the uncertainty: 'To die, and go we know not where.' He fears the thought of his living, breathing, emotional self becoming a lump of earth: 'This sensible warm motion to become a kneaded clod.' He fears hell, whether it is 'fiery floods' or 'thick-ribbed ice' or 'howling'. Even life at its worst, if he were to grow old and ill in jail ('age, ache, penury and imprisonment'), would be better than death. In the speech, the sequence of lines of ten syllables comes to an abrupt conclusion with a line of six, as though the last word inevitably comes too soon. Isabella responds, 'Alas, alas,' making up the missing four with a groan.

Measure for Measure is a comedy!

The title is taken from words of Jesus: 'Judge not, that ye be not judged. For with what judgment ye judge, ye shall be judged, and with what measure ye mete, it shall be measured unto you again.'[1] It has more references to the Bible than any other of Shakespeare's plays. It ends with judgement threatened but then is overwhelmed by forgiveness, which is why it is included among the comedies.

There are many marriages in the final scene but, as we have observed in other comic plays, not every one ends happily. Before the marriages there is a great deal of sex – enjoyed, forced, forbidden, innocent, foresworn or sold. The play went unperformed through stretches of history, but today it seems very current and is performed frequently. Directors find much to ask the audience to think about in its ambiguity.

The Duke of Vienna, a godly man called Vincentio, decides to see what happens if, instead of keeping absolute control over what his people do, he gives them free will. (So far, so Genesis.) He pretends to leave town, but actually disguises himself as a friar so that he can observe. He hands over power to Angelo, who is profoundly religious and puritanical.

Claudio is in deep trouble. The reason he is in prison is that he has got his girlfriend pregnant. They have actually had a civil marriage or betrothal of some kind, but have not had a church ceremony. Angelo, enforcing a pharisaic morality in relation to sex, demands his execution. The disguised Duke suggests that being reconciled to the prospect of death in the context of eternity enriches life. Claudio tells him, 'To sue to live, I find I seek to die, / And seeking death, find life. Let it come on.'[2] It is reminiscent of Jesus' words: 'He that will find his life, shall lose it: and he that loseth his life for my sake, shall find it.'[3] But Claudio's words are just the worthy sentiments he feels a Christian leader expects to hear. When the Duke is gone the truth comes pouring out in the speech we are looking at today.

Claudio has a sister, Isabella. She is a novice nun and sincerely full of faith. She goes to Angelo and begs him to spare her brother. Not only is she powerfully intelligent, she is also

---

1 Matthew 7.1–2.
2 Act 3, Scene 1.
3 Matthew 10.39.

gorgeous. Angelo is smitten. And the result is that he offers to release Claudio if she sleeps with him. Utter hypocrite!

So what will Isabella do? She absolutely refuses. In her Christian worldview, losing her virginity like this would mean eternal damnation. Her brother would lose his life, which would be tragic, but she would lose her eternal life, which would mean unending torture. As a teenager, her attitude seemed to me impossibly cruel; in this age of revelations about the abuses that powerful men commit, I am disposed to sympathize with any female character who refuses unwanted sex.

The stuff of comedy follows. The residents of a brothel give a bawdy commentary. A long-hidden spouse reappears. Angelo the trickster is comprehensively tricked. All the characters are manoeuvred into place so that the Duke can bring justice and order. They are veiled in order to create dramatic surprises. At the last minute it appears that all will be lost, but then the truth is revealed and the Duke insists that mercy will prevail. However, for today's culture, in which marriage is driven by love more than by the need for economic security, the 'happily ever after' ending is ambiguous and different productions can leave Isabella in bliss or facing a crisis.

'With what measure ye mete, it shall be measured unto you again.' Ironically, this is the play in which people do not get measure for measure. Instead they get mercy. Set in a Christian world of friars and nuns, it is a play about God's grace.

The hypocritical Angelo discovers this. When he is confronted by the Duke about his sins ('passes') he talks to him as if the Duke were God himself: 'O my dread lord! ... / I perceive your grace, like power divine / Hath look'd upon my passes.'[4] He begs for a quick death, because it is what he deserves. He doesn't get it. Instead he gets a reprieve and a wife. There is no revenge – it is the very opposite of *Titus Andronicus*. Is this how a play should end, with the innocent and guilty treated equally? The problem with mercy is that it is so unfair.

---

4 Act 5, Scene 1.

Unfair? Immediately after Jesus declared that his followers were not to judge one another in the Bible passage from which the play gets its title, he went on to lampoon our tendency to adopt a high moral stance against anyone except ourselves. We readily criticize someone with a speck of sawdust in their eye without dealing with the plank in our own (or as the Geneva Bible puts it, a mote and a beam).[5] The semi-blind are sitting in judgement on the partially sighted.

It is only when we grasp the seriousness of sin and our complete reliance on the forgiveness of God that we begin to experience true gratitude that God has chosen to show us mercy. And then the unfairness of mercy presents itself in a different light. As gratitude takes over our lives, the wells from which we draw in order to sustain us turn from bitter to sweet. The attitudes on which we depend in order to create our worldview turn from acid to revitalizing. Not only do we begin to see properly, but we begin to like what we see. Set free by the generosity of God, we look at other people generously. And when people recognize our generosity towards them, even those with whom we have had bruising experiences, joy has a chance. Even with the knowledge that death is inevitable, life, like this problematic play, is a divine comedy.

Jesus would have loved Claudio, with his groinful of sin but his frightened integrity. He would have hated Angelo, with his moral crusade but his self-pleasing hypocrisy. And yet, just like Duke Vincentio, he would have had mercy on both. That is the measure of his love for humankind in all its frailty.

---

5 Matthew 7.3–5.

Day 37

We are such stuff as dreams are made on

PROSPERO: Be cheerful, sir.
Our revels now are ended. These our actors,
As I foretold you, were all spirits and
Are melted into air, into thin air.
And like the baseless fabric of this vision,
The cloud-capped towers, the gorgeous palaces,
The solemn temples, the great globe itself –
Yea, all which it inherit – shall dissolve,
And like this insubstantial pageant faded,
Leave not a rack behind. We are such stuff
As dreams are made on, and our little life
Is rounded with a sleep.

The Tempest, Act 4, Scene 1

The Tempest is my favourite of Shakespeare's plays. (I may possibly have written something similar before!) It is usually assumed to be his final play – or, rather, the final play of which he was the sole author. This is a play through which reconciliation courses like a healing charm.

If you were to watch the plays of Shakespeare in order, somewhere near the beginning you would see *The Comedy of Errors*. It's a romp about twins who don't know each other exist. We looked at a speech from it last month: 'I to the world am like a drop of water / That in the ocean seeks another drop.'[1] It's about a young man's quest for identity. Who am I? Why am I? In this huge world will I ever find someone to love me? It all ends happily in an abbey, where a holy woman saves

1 *The Comedy of Errors*, Act 1, Scene 2.

the day. The play has a young man's optimism that we are in a world where we are all in the hands of an orderly God.

Twelve years later came the desolation of *King Lear*. The question at its heart is whether, when every trapping of civilized life is stripped away, there is anything left that makes a man or woman different from an animal. It's difficult to conclude from that play that there is a shred of dignity in being a human. Humanity is inches from a precipice beyond which there is no God, no soul, no hope and no compassion. 'Who is it that can tell me who I am?' asks the king.[2] It's one of a series of brilliant but bleak tragedies that William wrote in a short space of time. Even a comedy like *Measure for Measure*, written about the same time, includes a searing vision of hell, as we saw yesterday. There is no equivalent vision of heaven in any of the plays.

And then something changes. Shakespeare's final plays are flooded with compassion. *Pericles*, *A Winter's Tale* and *The Tempest* set up situations that might readily disintegrate into tragedy. But they don't. They step back from destruction because, in some way or another, an ancient magic intervenes. It is a magic that is never named, but that every Christian can recognize. People change. Forgiveness is possible. Reconciliation is possible. Wasted years can be redeemed.

The audience is flung into the tempest at the very start of the play. A ship is being wrecked. On board are Alonso, King of Naples, his son Ferdinand and Italian nobles. The King's Players almost certainly presented this in their indoor theatre at Blackfriars, meaning that fireworks and sound effects could fulfil the play's opening stage direction: 'Thunder and lightning heard.'

In the second scene, we meet Prospero and his daughter Miranda. We discover that Prospero is the brother of one of the people on board the boat – Antonio, the Duke of Milan. Twelve years earlier, Prospero had been the Duke. He had, however, become increasingly absorbed in learning magic and less in governing. His brother had usurped him. Left to die on a

2 *King Lear*, Act 1, Scene 4.

raft at sea, he washed up on an island, bringing with him only his daughter Miranda and his books of sorcery. Prospero has used his magic power to conjure up the storm, with the result that his enemies are now on the island and under his control.

Among them is Ferdinand, the king's son. He thinks he is the only survivor of the wreck. When he meets Miranda they immediately fall in love. But Prospero sets him to hard manual work in order to earn his approval for their romance.

A group including the king is also on the island. He is distraught because he thinks his son is dead. But he doesn't realize that he is under threat from his own noblemen, who are discussing how to seize the throne.

A butler and jester, becoming progressively drunker through the play, have also made it ashore and think that everyone else has drowned. They provide a comic subplot.

The island is not only full of beauty; it is full of non-human creatures. Ariel is a spirit with immense magical powers who serves Prospero in exchange for a promise that he will be set free. Caliban is the swarthy son of a witch and capable of both poetic dignity and monstrous behaviour. He was a native of the island before Prospero arrived – the magician enslaved him. (We are evidently meant to think of the Europeans who were colonizing much of the world in Shakespeare's day and recent productions have encouraged the audience to reflect uncomfortably on this.)

As Ariel leads the groups closer to their inevitable confrontation, the plotters against the King of Naples very nearly succeed in killing him. The butler and jester meet up with Caliban, who abases himself before them and talks them into a plan to overthrow Prospero. And the lovers' affection deepens into marriage, which is celebrated in a gorgeous, theatrical masquerade of supernatural creatures who dance to bless the couple.

It is as Prospero brings this masquerade to an end that he speaks the famous words we are looking at today. Some 130 years later, they were inscribed on Shakespeare's memorial in Westminster Abbey.

They are rather plaintive. They are about things coming to an end – a beautiful end, but an end nevertheless. Is he talking about theatre, or about the magical powers he is about to lay aside, or about life itself?

It is certainly about theatre, which conjures up a world at every performance that will never be precisely repeated once it is done. The reference to the globe is there to remind us of the Globe Theatre, which had been lost in a fire (a rack is a wisp of smoke). But it also reminds us of the fragility of the very planet we stand on.

The speech is about Prospero's magic too, because he has plans to leave the spellbinding island, bury his books and return to take up his responsibilities as a leader in Milan. In the final speech of the play, he tells us that without his powers of sorcery he is extremely weak and will put his trust in prayer. It is less beguiling in every way. But it is real.

And it is also about our very lives. Prospero subsequently tells us that when he returns to Italy 'every third thought shall be my grave'.[3] We are drawn into life from sleep, and at the end of it we return to sleep. It would be possible to lament this, but sleep is the place where dreams come from and, if that is all that life is, what gorgeous dreams we are made of.

Three short-lived things. But they are made all the more precious by the knowledge that they are fleeting. No wonder Prospero wants Ferdinand to 'be cheerful, sir'.

'New' is a key word in *The Tempest*. Its most notable use is when Miranda sees humans after 12 years of knowing only her father. 'O brave new world that has such people in't,' she gasps.[4]

So how does Prospero choose to spend the last of his magical moments? He could take revenge on those who wronged him all those years ago. He could punish Caliban for trying to kill him. He does neither of those things. Instead he makes things new. He forgives his brother, reconciles himself to his king,

---

3 Act 5, Scene 1.
4 Act 5, Scene 1.

frees Ariel from servitude, breaks his magic staff and bequeaths the island to Caliban.

The biblical character who Prospero most resembles is Joseph. He too is left for dead by his brothers, but survives and rises to a position of power. Far from perfect, he finds himself in a position where the life or death of his brothers is in his hands at a time of famine. He tests and taunts them in a cruel way. And then he reveals his identity and forgives them in a scene rich with tenderness: 'God sent me before you to preserve your posterity in this land, and to save you alive by a great deliverance.'[5]

However, the biblical theme that the play most exemplifies is grace. New, genuine, costly grace. This is the grace that is never far from our minds during this Holy Week. It has reconciled earth and heaven. It has reconciled human beings and God.

Yes, it is new, because it changes people. Grace allows people to decide that their future will no longer be imprisoned by their past. Paul wrote, 'If any man be in Christ, let him be a new creature. Old things are passed away: behold, all things are become new.'[6] In the goodness of God, this is a way that those whose lives have been tempestuous can choose. It is a brave new world.

Yes, it is genuine, because it is not escapist. Grace allows people to grow into the fullness of their potential. They leave behind island fantasies and walk in the world of reality. It's a reality in which life can be full of value and all the more so because we know we will one day leave it. Seen from the perspective of a loving God, we are such stuff as dreams are made on.

Yes, it is costly, because only the death of Jesus could bring it about. 'God was in Christ, and reconciled the world to himself, not imputing their sins unto them, and hath committed to us the word of reconciliation.'[7] Follow his steps during this

---

5 Genesis 45.7.
6 2 Corinthians 5.17.
7 2 Corinthians 5.19.

holiest of weeks as, tortured and alone, Jesus makes his way to the cross. Remember all over again the pain that brought forgiveness to the friends who deserted him. Recall the love that, through the centuries, made reunion with God possible for men and women who deserved nothing and received everything.

It was for you. You who have such storms and stresses in life that even at this moment your shoulders are tensed up under your ears. Someone was prepared to die for you because he found you to be so beautiful. You are reconciled to God and everything has changed. 'I have received a second life,' says Ferdinand.[8]

---

8 Act 5, Scene 1.

Day 38

A peace above all earthly dignities,
a still and quiet conscience

CROMWELL: How does your grace?
CARDINAL WOLSEY: Why, well;
Never so truly happy, my good Cromwell.
I know myself now; and I feel within me
A peace above all earthly dignities,
A still and quiet conscience. The king has cured me,
I humbly thank his grace; and from these shoulders,
These ruin'd pillars, out of pity, taken
A load would sink a navy, too much honour:
O 'tis a burthen, Cromwell, 'tis a burthen
Too heavy for a man that hopes for heaven!

Henry VIII, Act 3, Scene 2

In about 1611, William returned to Stratford-upon-Avon and made his home there. He repeatedly visited London after that and bought a house in Blackfriars near his indoor theatre, but 1609 had been a plague year and the theatres had been closed yet again. Whether for reasons of safety, creativity or wealth, his last five years were centred on Warwickshire. He owned property and a good deal of farmland there.

It was more profitable at the time to farm sheep for their wool than to use the land to grow wheat. Prosperous farmers fenced off enclosures for their sheep. The poor suffered as a result, with job losses and shortages of grain. Hungry people rioted. One would have hoped that William, whose compassion is a feature of so many plays, would have sided with the

poor. However, the documents that record his business deal-
ings at the time show him acting to protect his own wealth.

As he grew older, Shakespeare was increasingly collaborative
in his writing. *Henry VIII* was written jointly with a playwright
called John Fletcher and so was a play called *The Two Noble
Kinsmen*. Fletcher was a very successful writer, educated in
Cambridge and the son of the Bishop of London. Academics
use computerized analysis of the text to ascertain which scenes
are by which writer. Shakespeare has rich and distinctive traits
of language; Fletcher has elaborate stage directions.

It was one of those stage directions that was the play's
undoing. At the end of Act 1, dramatically splendid pageantry
accompanies a masked ball held in Cardinal Wolsey's palace.
During the performance on 29 June 1613, one of the cannons
misfired, a flame landed in the Globe Theatre's thatched roof
and the theatre burned to the ground.

The most important character in *Henry VIII* has no lines
and is still a baby at the end. It is Elizabeth I, who had cham-
pioned Shakespeare. She is baptized and Archbishop Thomas
Cranmer foresees her future greatness and the achievements
that her successors will have. Under her, Cranmer predicts,
'God shall be truly known.'[1] The play is about how obstacles
to the birth of the great queen are overcome. As if the point
were not obvious enough from the text, in Shakespeare's life-
time the play was not called *Henry VIII*, but *All Is True*.

At the beginning of the play, King Henry is married to his
first wife Katharine (Catherine of Aragon). Cardinal Wolsey
is a schemer who is manipulating international politics, but
at the same time acquiring wealth from lords who fall from
power through his machinations. It is in his interest to promote
relations with France and downgrade the influence of Spain.
So he plants the idea in Henry's mind that his marriage to
Katharine (daughter of the Spanish king) was illegal and intro-
duces him to beautiful young Anne Bullen (Boleyn, daughter of
the French king). Anne is to become Henry's second wife and
mother of Elizabeth.

---

1 Act 5, Scene 5.

In his way stands Buckingham, who sees through him. Wolsey has him arrested, tried on trumped-up charges and executed. The first obstacle is removed. However, the way Buckingham approaches his death is unexpected. There is no cursing, but a calm recognition that what is expected of a Christian is forgiveness: 'The law I bear no malice for my death; / 'T has done, upon the premises, but justice: / But those that sought it I could wish more Christians: / Be what they will, I heartily forgive 'em.'[2] It is another example of the grace of God bringing transformation at the end of a turbulent life that is typical of the plays that Shakespeare wrote at the end of his career.

The second downfall that occurs is that of Queen Katharine. Under the malign influence of Wolsey, Henry receives permission from the Pope to have the marriage annulled. Unlike Buckingham, Katharine does not go quietly. She protests that she has been an honourable wife for 20 years and now faces isolation and penury. But virtue is not the issue here. As far as the play is concerned, her crime is that she is not the mother of Elizabeth I, and so she has to go.

The third obstacle to be swept away is Wolsey himself. He falls because of his own inattention. Henry intercepts documents that reveal the extent to which Wolsey has profited from his manoeuvring and a letter from the Pope revealing that his part in the divorce negotiations was compromised. He is stripped of his titles and belongings.

However, he too is shown to be genuinely repentant. He makes 'a long farewell to all my greatness ... / Vain pomp and glory of this world I hate ye / I feel my heart new opened.' He urges his friend Cromwell to value honesty above corruption, to seek peace and to shun ambition (he makes reference to the Christian tradition that Satan was an angel who was cast out of God's presence for the sin of over-ambition). And he confesses how deeply he has let God down: 'Had I but served my

---

2 Act 2, Scene 1.

God with half the zeal / I served my king, he would not in mine age / Have left me naked to mine enemies.'[3]

The speech we are looking at today speaks of the blessing that comes from being at peace with God because you know that sins are forgiven. To have wrongdoing removed from your conscience is greater than all the honours which could be bestowed on you on earth ('all earthly dignities'). The burden of being aware that those honours were gained by underhand means was so weighty, says Wolsey, that it would sink not just a boat but a whole navy. However, 'I know myself now.'

Those who study these texts closely have noticed that the Cardinal's speeches in this scene use several words and phrases that occur in Psalm 34 as it is translated in the Geneva Bible and think Shakespeare may have been inspired by it. However, it is Psalm 32 that expresses most strongly the relief of knowing God's mercy:

> Blessed is he whose wickedness is forgiven, and whose sin
>   is covered ...
> When I held my tongue, my bones consumed, or when I
>   roared all the day ...
> Then I acknowledged my sin unto thee, neither hid I mine
>   iniquity:
> for I thought, I will confess against myself my wickedness
>   unto the Lord, and thou forgavest the punishment of
>   my sin.[4]

To say sorry is easy. To mean it is harder. To demonstrate it is hardest of all. The person who wrote the psalm had delayed too long in taking those steps. Unacknowledged shame had hung so heavily upon him that it impacted on his health physically (his 'bones') as well as mentally (he 'roared'). Not all sickness is by any means a result of sin. But all sin damages us as well as damaging those who suffer as a result of it and that needs to be addressed. This is the reason we set aside Lent as

---

3 Act 3, Scene 2.
4 Psalm 32.1, 3, 5.

a time for examining our lives. 'Remember you are dust and to dust you shall return. Turn away from sin and be faithful to Christ.'

The good news of the cross of Jesus Christ is threefold. It is the means by which we are forgiven, for it was there that the cost of that forgiveness was paid on our behalf. It is also the means by which we learn to forgive, for that is the example that Jesus set with his dying words. But there is a third reason why the news is incomparably good. It is because of the cross that we can come, over time, to forgive ourselves. In the words of the psalm: 'Be glad ye righteous.'[5] In the words Shakespeare gave to Cardinal Wolsey: 'Never so truly happy.'

We learn subsequently that Wolsey withdrew to a monastery, 'full of repentance', and died soon after. His are the words of a man who wants to be relieved of the burden of his failings because he 'hopes for heaven'. It is, of course, impossible to know whether they represent in any way the thoughts of Shakespeare as he wrote his last, or perhaps last but one, play. But in 1616, at home in Stratford-upon-Avon, he wrote his will.

---

5 Psalm 32.11.

Day 39

I commend my soul into the hands of God my Creator

In the name of God, Amen. I, William Shakespeare, in perfect
health and memory, God be praised, do ordain this my last
will and testament. First, I commend my soul into the hands
of God my Creator, hoping and assuredly believing, through
the only merits of Jesus Christ my Saviour, to be made
partaker of life everlasting, and I commend my body to the
earth whereof it is made.

William Shakespeare's will, 25 March 1616

William died on 23 April 1616, having caught a fever at a
'merry party' thrown by his fellow playwright Ben Jonson. He
was 52.

His will is preserved in the National Archive at Kew, near
London. In it he left the bulk of his estate to his eldest daughter
Susanna, who was married to a doctor and living in Stratford.
He left £300 to his younger daughter Judith, who had married
a scoundrel who was fined for committing adultery a month
after the wedding. He gave £10 to the poor of Stratford
which, compared to other wealthy landowners of the time,
was reasonably generous. And famously he left his wife Anne
'my second-best bed, with the furniture' (that is, the sheets and
blankets). Although this initially appears a slight, it was not an
unusual bequest. It is true, though, that unlike similar wills of
the time there is not one word of tenderness for the woman to
whom he had been married for 34 years, many of them spent
apart.

Most telling, however, is the way he faces death with confidence in Jesus Christ. The way it is put is typical of Protestant theology of the time, which casts doubt on the suggestion some make that he was secretly a Catholic. He bequeaths his body to the ground; he bequeaths his soul to his Saviour. He longs for eternal life, with his expectation poised between assured belief and optimistic hope (which, if we are honest, is the position most of us are in). And he knows that this is possible solely because of all that Jesus has done for him (his 'only merits') on the cross.

The final week of Lent, Holy Week, is the point at which our attention turns to death and in particular the tragic and appalling death of Jesus. These are hard things to think about. We do not want to dwell on death. Not ours; not anybody's.

The biggest challenge of the week is to see Jesus' death through the eyes of his first followers, who (unlike us) did not know what was to come. All they knew was that their friend was dying young and in great pain. Their dream that he would be the one who would change the destiny of their homeland had come to nothing. They undoubtedly recalled that Jesus had warned them with increasing regularity that, as a result of what he was doing, his death was certain. But nothing in the Gospels suggests that, as they watched the crucifixion, they were clinging on to or even half-remembering words about his death not being the end.

One of the reasons that spending Lent in the company of Shakespeare is valuable is that he makes us think about death when our instinct is to put it out of our minds. There are some things you can do to consider your death in a positive way. The first is to put your affairs in order, as he did. Then ensure that there is nothing unsaid in the relationships that have been significant in your life. Make peace. Be sure that you are not leaving those you care for with a second-best bedful of regrets.

Be honest about realities. There are questions that everyone asks as their life comes to a close, so don't hold back from talking about them. Why is this happening now? What has my life been for? Who am I? These are the questions of Lear,

Prospero, Hamlet and Rosalind. These are the questions of Paul, Martha, Job and the writers of the psalms.

And say goodbye. Say it with its true meaning: 'God be with ye.'

In the twenty-first century, we are notably unwilling to engage with the realities of death. But people did not want to do so 2,000 years ago either.

A young, wealthy man sought Jesus' advice because he didn't want to die. He thought Jesus might be able to help him and so he came with his questions prepared. He was immensely polite: 'There came one running, and kneeled to him, and asked him, "Good Master, what shall I do, that I may possess eternal life?" Jesus said to him, "Why callest thou me good? There is none good but one, even God."'[1]

It has to be said that Jesus was teasing him. He had met people like this young man before and recognized a genuine desire to be good. The man then set himself the unattainable target of perfection. He implied that he would keep every single commandment perfectly and with no failures if the result was that he would never die. You can imagine Jesus trying to keep a straight face as he recognized both the sincerity and absurdity of the man's intentions. A flood of affection for him flowed out of Jesus. But that didn't stop him coming out with the most challenging words he ever uttered: 'One thing is lacking unto thee. Go and sell all that thou hast, and give to the poor, and thou shalt have treasure in heaven, and come, follow me.'[2]

As they watched the dejected man walk away, Jesus' disciples were bewildered. 'Who then can be saved?' they asked. And Jesus' answer was dazzling. 'With men it is impossible, but not with God: for with God all things are possible.'[3] For a man or woman to live again after their death is unthinkable. It simply cannot happen. It would take an unparalleled miracle. But that miracle is the very same miracle that raised Jesus from the dead. That miracle happens.

1 Mark 10.17–18.
2 Mark 10.21.
3 Mark 10.27.

This is the way to prepare for a good death. Denying it does not help in any way. Striving to earn a life after you die by your achievements is futile. However, this you can hope and assuredly believe – when the time comes to die, all you need to do is die. Truly, that is all. 'Through the only merits of Jesus Christ my Saviour', God will do absolutely everything else that is required. He will work the miracle.

I work for the Church of England and, some years ago, the job took me to Holy Trinity Church in Stratford-upon-Avon. Standing with the vicar at the back of the church talking about mission, my attention was drawn to a woman kneeling in front of the altar, hunched and quietly crying. After a while she got up, sorted herself out and turned to go. As she passed the vicar she said in an American accent, 'I just don't know where I would be without that man.'

Because of my job I am used to people saying that to me about Jesus. But as we walked to the east end of the church, I realized that she had been in front of Shakespeare's gravestone. I've never been sure since whether she was worshipping Jesus or William. One or other of them has given her something that sustains her in life. Sometimes the memory unsettles me and sometimes it makes me smile. Shakespeare is not the Resurrection and the Life (that's one of Jesus' sayings). But I'm pleased that the hope he's given to the woman has been a tower of strength (that's one of Shakespeare's).

For those who love Shakespeare, his legacy is a source of comfort and it sustains them in darkness and on days when death seems to have the final word. For those who love Jesus, an incomparably different prospect upholds them. Easter is coming.

Day 40

It is required you do awake your faith

(Paulina draws a curtain, and discovers Hermione, standing like a statue.)

PAULINA: Quit presently the chapel, or resolve you
For more amazement. If you can behold it,
I'll make the statue move indeed, descend
And take you by the hand; but then you'll think –
Which I protest against – I am assisted
By wicked powers.
LEONTES: What you can make her do,
I am content to look on: what to speak,
I am content to hear; for 'tis as easy
To make her speak as move.
PAULINA: It is required
You do awake your faith. Then all stand still;
On: those that think it is unlawful business
I am about, let them depart.
LEONTES: Proceed:
No foot shall stir.
PAULINA: Music, awake her; strike! *(Music plays.)*
'Tis time; descend; be stone no more; approach.
Strike all that look upon with marvel. Come,
I'll fill your grave up: stir, nay, come away,
Bequeath to death your numbness, for from him
Dear life redeems you. You perceive she stirs.
(Hermione comes down.)
Start not; her actions shall be holy as
You hear my spell is lawful: do not shun her
Until you see her die again; for then
You kill her double. Nay, present your hand:

When she was young you wooed her; now in age
Is she become the suitor?
LEONTES: O, she's warm!
If this be magic, let it be an art
Lawful as eating.

The Winter's Tale, Act 5, Scene 3

You have just read about a resurrection. Nothing less! *The Winter's Tale* is a remarkable play from the very end of Shakespeare's writing life. It has within it, I believe, the most beautiful line that Shakespeare ever wrote. It's not, 'Exit, pursued by a bear,' which is the stage direction that challenges directors and entertains audiences.[1] It is altogether simpler and more telling than that, as we shall see.

Everything about the first half of the play is ice and bitterness. 'A sad tale's best for winter,' says Mamillius, a child who doesn't realize that his life is about to be cut short.[2] We are led to anticipate a raw tragedy.

Leontes, king of Sicilia, and Polixenes, king of Bohemia, have been best friends since childhood. Leontes' wife Hermione is pregnant and very fond of Polixenes. But inside the king an irrational jealousy is growing and he mistakes the friendship between the two for an affair. His jealousy explodes into an accusation that the baby Hermione is carrying belongs to Polixenes, forcing him to flee back to his home.

Leontes has his wife thrown in jail. There she gives birth to a girl. Her companion Paulina brings the baby to Leontes and pleads with him to reconsider. But his paranoia is surging and he orders the baby to be taken away and abandoned in a far-flung place.

Hermione is put on trial and Leontes declares her guilty. But at that moment a message arrives. The Oracle of Delphi (the high priestess of the Temple of Apollo in Greece, whose

---

1 Act 3, Scene 3.
2 Act 2, Scene 1.

pronouncements were trusted utterly) has made a judgement. Hermione and Polixenes are blameless and the king is a jealous tyrant. Leontes' frozen heart refuses to accept it, but a servant rushes in with news that his son Mamillius has died from the burden of his father's cruelty. Hermione collapses and is carried away. Leontes is overcome with grief and descends into despair when Paulina informs him that his wife has also died. Leontes vows that the rest of his life will be spent in penance for the sin he now recognizes. The tragic chill of this tale of winter is complete.

But what of the baby that he so cruelly banished? She is taken to Bohemia where she is left with proof of her identity and a chest of gold. (It is the unfortunate man who whisks her away that has the fatal encounter with a bear.) She is found by a shepherd, who takes her home and gives her the name Perdita (it means 'lost').

Sixteen years later she is gorgeous and has caught the attention of Florizel, who happens to be the son of King Polixenes. In the altogether different atmosphere of Bohemia, the bitterness of the first half of the play begins to transform. A springtime sheep-shearing festival brings on to the stage colour, dance and a variety of rogues and people in disguise. Among them is Polixenes, who has disguised himself to find out what his son is up to. He is furious when he finds him dating Perdita, who is far too lowly to be in the company of a prince. But Florizel wants to marry the girl he loves and they take flight. They board a boat bound for Sicilia, with all the major characters in pursuit.

After all these years, Leontes is still grieving. A chastened man, he speaks of the gods, heaven, sin and the blessing that follows repentance. The entrance of Prince Florizel with his beautiful wife lifts his spirits and reminds him of his old friend. To his delight, Polixenes then arrives in person and, when the shepherd tells the story of how he found the baby, both kings realize Perdita's true identity and there is much rejoicing.

But that is not the end of the story. In the chapel of Paulina's house there is a statue of Hermione so realistic that it even has wrinkles as if she had aged 16 years since we last saw her. Invited there to see it, Leontes is overcome and this is where the scene we are looking at today unfolds.

Paulina tells the awed Leontes that she can make the statue move, but she is reluctant to do so because he will think that 'wicked powers' are being invoked, when the reverse is true. In order for his restoration to be complete, he must have faith.

Leontes assents. The statue stirs. Hermione lives. Whether she has spent all those years alive but in hiding or whether this is a resurrection from the dead is not made clear. What is clear, however, is that death has been defeated and grace has flooded what we expected to be a tragedy with joy. Paulina tells the statue that it is time to shake off the stillness ('numbness') of death and be redeemed into new life: 'Bequeath to death your numbness, for from him / Dear life redeems you.'

This scene ought not to work, because it is so preposterous. And yet in a theatre, bewitchingly lit and underscored with music, its magic ambushes an audience with emotion time after time. How does Shakespeare prompt tears at that point? With the most beautiful line he ever wrote. Leontes reaches out to touch his living wife and whispers: 'Oh, she's warm.'

First a gasp, and then two simple monosyllables. In them is a world of wonder. There is astonished recognition that this is not an apparition but a living being. There is a sigh of delight in human touch. And all that ice, all that bitterness which had Leontes in its grip for years and years is melting. The winter's tale is over. He has found warmth.

The man who wrote this is the same man who sent King Lear, a 'poor, bare, fork'd animal', naked into a storm.[3] It is the same man who allowed Othello to be so beset by jealousy (the very sin that undid Leontes) that the play ends in a frenzy of death.[4] Something happened! Something must have happened to William towards the end of his life which meant that he couldn't bring himself to sustain the cynicism that drove the great tragedies and instead filled his final plays with forgive-

---

3 *King Lear*, Act 3, Scene 4.
4 *Othello*, Act 5, Scene 2.

ness and restoration. Nobody knows what it was and it's likely that nobody ever will.

This is the play in which all's well that ends well, much more so than the play to which he gave that title. And, although the name of Jesus is not mentioned, anyone who has experienced for themselves the grace of the Christian good news can recognize what it is that stops the course of what should be a tragedy and instead leads it into a place of healing.

First, there is a good shepherd, who finds and saves a girl who has been named 'Lost'. This is a clear reference to the parable Jesus told about a shepherd who leaves 99 sheep and goes searching for one that has gone astray. When the story is told in Matthew's Gospel, Jesus explains that it is about God's longing for men and women that tragedy should not prevail: 'So is it not the will of your Father, which is in heaven, that one of these little ones should perish.'[5]

It isn't obvious what kind of religious landscape the play is set in. In some ways it is a pagan world where characters believe in Greek gods and revere the Oracle. Bohemia is in Central Europe and has had a troubled religious history, but in the play it feels more like rural England because Christians are celebrating Pentecost with 'Whitsun pastorals'. Sicilia is in Catholic Italy and that is where Leontes speaks of remorse and repentance. But Paulina insists that no action of his own, even if he were to pray on his knees on a snow-blasted mountain, will earn him the forgiveness he seeks: 'A thousand knees / Ten thousand years together, naked, fasting / Upon a barren mountain and still winter / In storm perpetual, could not move the gods.'[6] His hope lies in the compassion of God alone.

Faith is what saves Leontes. 'It is required you do awake your faith,' Paulina tells him. He has lived in a world in which he has isolated himself from everyone in the court and attempted to find fulfilment in the power he has to control the world around him. It has brought him no joy. He needs to acknowledge that there is something supernatural in the world that

5 Matthew 18.14.
6 Act 3, Scene 2.

he cannot control. Someone whose 'actions shall be holy'. He needs the intervention of what Christians know to be a good and gracious God.

Numb in that arctic need, Leontes touches resurrection.

Seven days after Jesus rose from the dead, his friend Thomas also knew the numbness with which grief constricts your world. Still unaware that something profoundly supernatural had overturned all concepts of what is possible, he declared, 'Except I see in his hands the print of the nails, and put my finger into the print of the nails, and put mine hand into his side, I will not believe it.'[7]

In the depth of that pain, Jesus chose to reveal himself. He came with words of peace. He came with reassurance that what Thomas needed at that moment would be granted to him: 'Put forth thine hand.'[8] Jesus was there not as an apparition but as a moving, touchable, breathing reality. And in that moment of touch, Thomas' faith awoke: 'Thou art my Lord and my God.'[9]

Easter is at hand. William Shakespeare's birthday will follow soon after, but Easter will come first. This chill world of hurt and damage needs to be overwhelmed with grace. The winter of our proud human hearts needs a Saviour. Our little loves and frozen hopes need to live once more. Reach out to Jesus in whom there is grace and love and life. Oh, he will be warm!

It is required you do awake your faith.

---

7 John 20.25.
8 John 20.27.
9 John 20.28.